Business and Industry

EDITORS

William R. Childs
Scott B. Martin
Wanda Stitt-Gohdes

VOLUME 7

MICROECONOMICS to
PHILIP MORRIS COMPANIES

MARSHALL CAVENDISH
NEW YORK · TORONTO · LONDON · SYDNEY

Marshall Cavendish
99 White Plains Road
Tarrytown, New York 10591-9001

www.marshallcavendish.com

© 2004 Marshall Cavendish Corporation

Library of Congress Cataloging-in-Publication Data

Business and industry / editors, William R. Childs, Scott B. Martin, Wanda Stitt-Gohdes.
        p. cm.
    Includes bibliographical reference and index.
    Contents: v. 1. Accounting and Bookkeeping to Burnett, Leo--v. 2. Business Cycles to Copyright--
v. 3. Corporate Governance to Entrepreneurship--v. 4. Environmentalism to Graham,
Katharine--v. 5. Great Depression to Internship--v. 6. Inventory to Merrill Lynch--
v. 7. Microeconomics to Philip Morris Companies--v. 8. Price Controls to Sarnoff, David--
v. 9. Savings and Investment Options to Telecommuting--v. 10. Temporary Workers to Yamaha--
v. 11. Index volume
    ISBN 0-7614-7430-7 (set)--ISBN 0-7614-7437-4 (v. 7)
        1. Business--Encyclopedias. 2. Industries--Encyclopedias. I. Childs, William R., 1951-II. Martin,
  Scott B., 1961-III. Stitt-Gohdes, Wanda.

HF1001 .B796 2003
338'.003--dc21   2002035156

Printed in Italy

06 05 04 03 5 4 3 2 1

MARSHALL CAVENDISH
Editorial Director   Paul Bernabeo
Production Manager   Alan Tsai

Produced by The Moschovitis Group, Inc.

THE MOSCHOVITIS GROUP
President, Publishing Division   Valerie Tomaselli
Executive Editor   Hilary W. Poole
Associate Editor   Sonja Matanovic
Design and Layout   Annemarie Redmond
Illustrator   Richard Garratt
Assistant Illustrator   Zahiyya Abdul-Karim
Photo Research   Gillian Speeth
Production Associates   K. Nura Abdul-Karim, Rashida Allen
Editorial Assistants   Christina Campbell, Nicole Cohen, Jessica Rosin
Copyediting   Carole Campbell
Proofreading   Paul Scaramazza
Indexing   AEIOU, Inc.

Alphabetical Table of Contents

Microeconomics

Economics is the study of how societies use scarce resources to produce goods and services and how societies distribute those goods and services. Resources—land, natural resources, and labor, as well as machines, tools, and buildings—are scarce because people want more goods and services than there are resources and abilities to produce them. Given this fundamental condition of scarcity, economic efficiency becomes an important concept. A society is economically efficient if resources are being used to make itself as well off as possible. These two concepts, scarcity and economic efficiency, underlie all of economics.

Economics has been traditionally divided into two areas: microeconomics and macroeconomics, with *micro* meaning "small" and *macro* meaning "large." Macroeconomics considers the behavior of the economy as a whole; microeconomics is the study of individual consumers, workers, and producers functioning in specific markets. Microeconomics topics include: the behavior and decision making of individuals and businesses; how their decisions affect themselves and society; how the kind of market that is formed affects prices, profits, and production within the market; how the incomes are determined; and the appropriate economic role of government in influencing the use and distribution of resources. Microeconomics explores how those markets function and generate or do not generate efficient outcomes for society. It also considers where markets can fail and suggests solutions to improve market efficiency and fairness.

For example, the number of personal computers a company and an industry produce is a microeconomic issue, but the total amount of output of all goods and services in the economy is a macroeconomic issue. Pricing of personal computers is a microeconomic topic, while the rate of change in prices of all goods and services produced in an economy is a macroeconomic topic.

Changes in unemployment rates of high school dropouts fall within the confines of microeconomics, but the causes of changes in unemployment rates for all individuals are analyzed by macroeconomics. Although microeconomists may study large markets and large companies, they are still individual markets and companies.

Adam Smith, whose *The Wealth of Nations* was published in 1776, is the founder of microeconomics. He examined how the prices of goods, services, and resources are determined, and the strengths and weaknesses of different markets. In particular, he discussed the effectiveness of markets where individuals pursue their own self-interests. He also explored how markets can fail to be efficient.

The Basics of Microeconomics

Microeconomics begins with an examination of the fundamental economic problem—scarcity. Given scarcity, choices must be made about how resources are used. Microeconomics focuses on the consequences of the choices made by individuals, firms, and governments, and evaluates those decisions for their effectiveness in making consumers, workers, businesses, and all of society as well off as possible.

The microeconomic concept of comparative advantage explains why individuals and businesses benefit when they specialize and trade. If individuals specialize instead of trying to produce everything they need or want, two consequences result. Total production in a society increases, but each individual becomes dependent upon others. To consume goods and services other than the ones they produce, the specializing

See also:
Comparative Advantage;
Macroeconomics; Monopoly;
Opportunity Cost; Public
Goods; Supply and Demand.

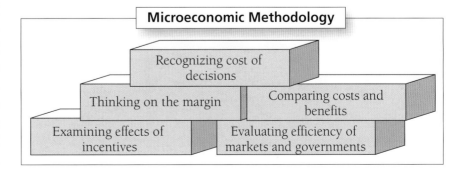

Microeconomic Methodology

Recognizing cost of decisions

Thinking on the margin

Comparing costs and benefits

Examining effects of incentives

Evaluating efficiency of markets and governments

Determinants of Supply and Demand	
Supply	**Demand**
• Technology changes	• Price of the good
• Cost factors of production	• Desire for the good
• Prices of other goods	• Income of consumer
• Taxes	• Availability and price of other goods
• Expectations about prices	
• Number of sellers	• Expectations for income and prices

individuals must trade for the other goods and services they want. That trade takes place in markets. How those markets work is at the heart of microeconomics. Microeconomic principles are the same for local, national, and international markets and in markets for goods and services, labor, land, financial instruments, currencies, and other resources.

The analysis of markets begins with an exploration of supply and demand. Economists study how firms make decisions about how to set prices and quantities to produce. The supply side of any market depends upon costs and availability of productive resources and the technology that is available to firms. Once these are determined, firms can decide whether and how much to produce based on their costs compared with the prices they can receive in the market. Consumers, in efforts to maximize their own well-being, decide whether to purchase goods and services. The decision of how much to buy depends upon the price of the goods and services as well as the consumers' tastes, incomes, and available alternatives. The market outcome—price and quantity of the good or service—results from the interaction of both sides of the market.

Whether a market is economically efficient is highly dependent upon market structure. Much of microeconomics concentrates on development of one model that describes a perfectly competitive market, a market with many buyers and sellers, much knowledge about prices and qualities, a homogeneous product, and relatively easy entry and exit by firms into the market. The opposite extreme is a market with only a single producer—a monopoly. The outcomes, in terms of economic efficiency, of those two markets are quite different. The perfectly competitive market most often provides an economically efficient use of resources, while the monopolist will charge a higher price, produce less, and not have the incentives to hold costs to the lowest possible levels.

Between these two extremes is oligopoly, market models with only a few producers, and monopolistic competition, markets with many producers, each one producing its own unique product. A useful tool, game theory, is often used to analyze firm behavior in these markets. Game theory is used to explore how individuals and firms act when their actions affect other individuals and firms, which, in turn, can cause a reaction by the other individuals and firms, which affects the outcome of the initial decision. Tools like game theory, along with cost-benefit comparisons, are important practical parts of research and decision making.

Another aspect of microeconomics is the study of factors of production (labor, land, natural resources, and capital) and resulting income distribution. Through application of the appropriate supply and demand tools, the process of determining prices, and therefore incomes, can be understood.

Microeconomics and Politics

Out of the analysis of markets comes an economic role for government. Although portions of the economic role of government fall within macroeconomics, a substantial economic role for government exists that is directly connected with individual, firm, and market behavior. If markets are not competitive, for example, they

Example of Gains from Specialization				
	Unspecialized production capability (units)		Specialized production capability (units)	
	Product 1	Product 2	Product 1	Product 2
Company A	50	40	76	30
Company B	19	34	13	58
Total production	69	74	89	88

are not efficient. Thus, one economic role for government is antitrust regulation aimed at encouraging competition, holding prices down, promoting innovation, and providing economically efficient results. In other cases, competition may not work perfectly because consumers do not have the ability to understand the product fully—prescription drugs, for example—or where a monopoly can actually produce goods or services at lower costs than competitive firms, as with many public utilities. Here, the role of the government is regulatory.

Governments also produce some goods and services that a market cannot produce in economically efficient amounts. Often businesses in such markets would earn a profit only with great difficulty. Therefore, the amount produced would be less than economically efficient. National defense is one example. A private firm may not be able to set a price because, if national defense already exists, everyone is protected whether they choose to be or not. Many individuals would not buy the services, and businesses would have to contract, and perhaps disappear.

In other cases, governments produce or subsidize goods that offer external benefits.

External benefits are those received by individuals other than those directly involved in producing or consuming the good. Public education and research and development in basic science are good examples. In these cases, buyers will tend to not purchase an amount sufficient for economic efficiency because they do not pay attention to the extra benefits received by others (or are unaware of those benefits). Only through government subsidies or production can an economy come closer to an efficient level of production in these areas.

Governments may find it necessary to tax or regulate how other goods are produced when external costs exist. The best example is when significant pollution is created in a production process. External costs (the pollution itself) are borne by individuals other than those directly involved in producing or consuming the good or service. As a result, too much of the good or service is produced, as businesses and consumers do not pay all of the costs. Only if government adopts regulations or taxes business will businesses adjust their production levels or methods.

All of these government activities must be paid for, and market economies normally

The Free Electron Laser, developed at the Los Alamos National Laboratory in New Mexico; relying on the private sector to provide national defense and pure scientific research can be economically inefficient, so governments frequently provide subsidies.

The waste produced by this petrochemical plant is an external cost that is borne by the society as a whole, rather than the chemical producers themselves. Governments regulate waste-producers in order to force them to keep these external costs under control.

use taxes to do so. The effect of the taxation on incentives to work, produce, and save—and therefore on economic efficiency—is another part of microeconomics.

Incentives are a fundamental part of economics not only for firms and individuals, but for governments also. Government decision making often involves incentives different from those of consumers and producers. As a result, governments can make decisions that are not economically efficient, a situation characterized by microeconomics as a government failure. Microeconomics includes analysis of the effects of government policy decisions that influence markets by setting minimum prices (for wages, as an example)

and maximum prices (rent controls in some areas) in markets for labor and tariffs and quotas on imported goods and services.

Microeconomics is a method of thinking about issues. Microeconomics, with its methodology of recognizing the costs of decisions, thinking on the margin, comparing costs and benefits, examining the effects of incentives, and evaluating economic efficiency of markets and governments, is the core of all of economic analysis. Microeconomics focuses those tools and methods on how societies organize their resources to produce and then distribute goods and services.

Themes in Microeconomics

- Behavior and decision making of individuals and businesses
- How decisions of businesses and individuals affect themselves and society
- How the kinds of markets formed affect prices, profits, and production within the market
- How incomes are determined
- The appropriate economic role of government in influencing the distribution of resources

Further Reading

Baumol, William J., and Alan S. Blinder. *Microeconomics: Principles and Policy.* 8th ed. Fort Worth, Tex.: Dryden Press, Harcourt College Publishers, 2000.

Breit, William, and Roger L. Ransom. *The Academic Scribblers.* 3rd ed. Princeton, N.J.: Princeton University Press, 1998.

Glahe, Fred R., ed. *Adam Smith's* An Inquiry into the Nature and Causes of the Wealth of Nations, A Concordance. Savage, Md.: Rowman & Littlefield, 1993.

Heilbroner, Robert L. *The Worldly Philosophers: The Lives, Times, and Ideas of the Great Economic Thinkers.* Rev. 7th ed. New York: Simon & Schuster, 1999.

—Stephen Buckles

Microsoft

With annual revenues greater than $14 billion, Microsoft is more than the largest software company in the world: It is a cultural phenomenon. Founded by Bill Gates and Paul Allen, Microsoft develops, manufactures, and licenses software products, technology, and services. Virtually every personal computer in the world contains at least one Microsoft product. The company's aggressive business tactics have inspired repeated lawsuits and antitrust proceedings.

The Birth of Microsoft

Gates and Allen, both fascinated by computers, met as high school students in Seattle. While still in high school, Gates and Allen both worked for the Computer Center Corporation and for the defense contractor TRW. In 1972 they started their first company, Traf-O-Data, which sold a rudimentary computer that recorded and analyzed traffic data. The project earned them about $20,000.

In the fall of 1973 Allen went to the University of Washington to study computer science and Gates enrolled at Harvard. In December 1974 Allen was on his way to visit Gates when he stopped to pick up a copy of *Popular Electronics*. The lead article was about a new computer kit, the Altair 8080; its title: "World's First Microcomputer Kit to Rival Commercial Models." A few days later, Gates called Micro Instrumentation and Telemetry Systems (MITS), the makers of the Altair. He told the company that he and Allen had developed software that could be used on the Altair. In truth, neither of them even owned an Altair, but they managed to write the code in just eight weeks. MITS was impressed and bought the rights to their program.

Later that year, Gates left Harvard (Allen had already dropped out) to work full time as director of software development for MITS. At the same time, Gates and Allen formed a company of their own to develop other programs. They named their partnership MicroSoft (changing the spelling not long after). Their total revenues for 1975 were $16,000.

In November 1976 Allen left MITS to devote his full attention to his own company. Microsoft swiftly became a leading distributor for microcomputer programming languages. By the end of 1978 Microsoft had 13 employees, a sales subsidiary in Japan, and $1 million in revenues.

The Birth of DOS

In 1980 IBM was frantically working to develop a microcomputer of its own. The mainframe manufacturer had been left behind in the microcomputer revolution and was scrambling to make up lost ground. IBM gave Microsoft the contract to write a new operating system for the IBM personal computer (PC). What Gates and Allen eventually produced was the Microsoft Disk Operating System, or MS-DOS. This system was based entirely on an operating system called QDOS

See also:
Computer Industry;
Gates, Bill; IBM; Internet;
Sherman Antitrust Act.

Microsoft cofounders Paul Allen (left) and Bill Gates in 1984.

(Quick and Dirty Operating System), written by Tim Paterson of Seattle Computer Products. Microsoft bought the rights to QDOS for $50,000, then modified the program for IBM and renamed it MS-DOS. Gates negotiated a deal with IBM that allowed Microsoft to retain the rights to MS-DOS; thus Microsoft would earn a fee for every computer sold.

That deal was to be the making of Microsoft. The cheap and reliable IBM PC took off immediately, becoming the standard for the huge PC industry. When other manufacturers began building PC clones, they also leased the rights to MS-DOS from Microsoft. In 1981 the company was incorporated as Microsoft, Inc., with Gates as president and chairman and Allen as executive vice president. The company ended the year with 128 employees and revenues of $16 million. In 1983 Allen left Microsoft after being diagnosed with Hodgkin's disease.

Microsoft moved to a new corporate headquarters in Redmond, Washington, in 1986 and went public in March of that year. The initial public offering of 2.5 million shares raised $61 million. Within a year, the stock price had risen from $25 per share to $85. Bill Gates became a billionaire at age 31, and many of Microsoft's employees, who had accepted lower wages in exchange for stock options, also became millionaires.

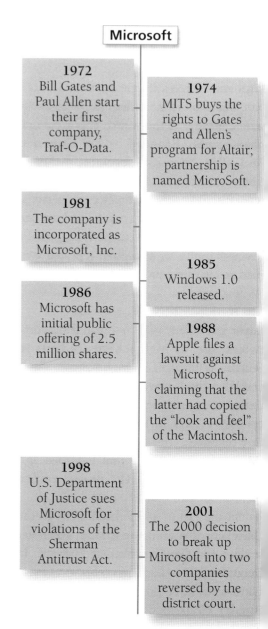

Microsoft

1972
Bill Gates and Paul Allen start their first company, Traf-O-Data.

1974
MITS buys the rights to Gates and Allen's program for Altair; partnership is named MicroSoft.

1981
The company is incorporated as Microsoft, Inc.

1985
Windows 1.0 released.

1986
Microsoft has initial public offering of 2.5 million shares.

1988
Apple files a lawsuit against Microsoft, claiming that the latter had copied the "look and feel" of the Macintosh.

1998
U.S. Department of Justice sues Microsoft for violations of the Sherman Antitrust Act.

2001
The 2000 decision to break up Mircosoft into two companies reversed by the district court.

Windows for the World

In 1984 Apple introduced its Macintosh computer. Instead of typed commands, the Mac used a graphical user interface (GUI) based on icons. Now even complete novices could use the computer, simply by moving the cursor to an icon and clicking. Microsoft had worked closely with Apple during the Mac's development, and soon introduced Mac versions of its programs. As the Mac became popular, Microsoft saw its earnings jump—from $50 million in 1983 to nearly $100 million in 1984.

At the same time, Microsoft began developing a GUI of its own, one that would work with MS-DOS, dubbed Windows. When Windows 1.0 was released in November

1985, it was slow, could run only a few programs, and was full of bugs. This began what Microsoft critics complain is a long-running trend. In January 2002 Brent Schlender wrote in *Fortune*, "From its beginnings, Microsoft has been notorious for producing inelegant products that are frequently inferior and bringing them to the market way behind schedule." However, as Mitchell Kertzman, CEO of Liberate Technologies, warned in 2001, "Eventually [Microsoft engineers] figure it out. If you assume that they won't catch up, they've got you. You're cooked."

The improved 2.0 version of Windows released in December of 1987, made the PC look a lot like the Macintosh. In 1988 Apple filed a lawsuit against Microsoft, alleging that Microsoft had copied the "look and feel" of the Macintosh, breaking the 1985 licensing agreement and infringing on 170 Apple copyrights. Four years later, the U.S. District Court ruled that the licensing agreement gave Microsoft the rights to use all but nine of the copyrights. A later ruling stated that the remaining infringements were not covered by copyright law at all.

Windows 95 was released in August 1995, selling one million copies in the first four days. Microsoft's Windows 95 licensing agreement required every computer using Windows 95 to come with Microsoft's own Internet browser, Internet Explorer 4, already installed—an arrangement that would later lead to antitrust trouble for Microsoft. Windows 98, released in June of 1998, was the last version of Windows based on MS-DOS.

Microsoft vs. the Rest of the World

Microsoft's critics argued that the company stifled software innovation by using its power to squeeze out competitors. Most famously, when Microsoft required all computers using Windows to carry Internet Explorer, Microsoft ended Netscape Navigator's reign as the most popular Internet browser. Critics charged that by forcing out competing browsers, Microsoft was controlling access to the Internet. In May 1998 the U.S. Department of Justice and 17 states sued Microsoft for violations of the Sherman Antitrust Act. The government claimed that Microsoft had entered into anticompetitive agreements with computer manufacturers by forcing the manufacturers to include Internet Explorer with the Windows 95 operating system; and that Microsoft used exclusive agreements with Internet service and content providers, including America Online, to bolster its market share and force out competitors.

The trial began on October 19, 1998. On November 5, 1999, U.S. District Court Justice Thomas Penfield Jackson ruled that Microsoft was a monopoly. On April 3, 2000, Jackson found that Microsoft had violated the Sherman Antitrust Act. Later that month, the Justice Department proposed that Microsoft be split into two companies and be subject to a number of business-conduct restrictions. Jackson agreed and on June 7, he ordered the split. Microsoft appealed the decision. The appeal was heard before a Washington, D.C., district court judge, who on June 28, 2001, reversed the breakup order, finding that the company did illegally attempt to maintain its monopoly on Intel-based PC operating systems but did not illegally attempt to monopolize the market for Web browsers. Although the breakup was averted, the door was left open for future antitrust suits.

The Future of Microsoft, the Future of Computing

By the late 1990s Microsoft had lost a lot of its market share. As the future of computing moved online, Microsoft seemed to have missed the revolution. However, Microsoft was determined to dominate the online industry as it dominated the PC software industry. Heavy with cash, Microsoft has

Bill Gates testifies before the U.S. Senate in 1999.

Microsoft is the biggest software provider in the world; here, shoppers browse through Microsoft products in the Akihabara shopping district in Tokyo.

plowed money into software development and acquisitions, making inroads into the lucrative market for the server software that runs Web sites. After a shaky start, Microsoft's MSN Web services (including the MSN portal, Hotmail, MSNBC, and other Web sites) have more combined traffic worldwide than the collective properties of either Yahoo! or America Online.

In 2001 Microsoft launched a number of new products: Stinger, a new operating system for cell phones; Xbox, a game console; and Windows XP, a new version of the desktop operating system. Microsoft plans to connect everything it makes with a new kind of technology, called .Net, that will allow consumers and companies to access and run any kind of application on the Internet from any device. Microsoft has been

building .Net technology into nearly all of its products and services. As a result, all of Microsoft's PC software will become Web services that can be rented and downloaded from the Internet.

Further Reading

Auletta, Ken. *World War 3.0: Microsoft and Its Enemies.* New York: Random House, 2001.

Margolis, Stephen E., and Stanley J. Liebowitz. *Winners, Losers & Microsoft: Competition and Antitrust in High Technology.* Oakland, Calif.: Independent Institute, 2001.

Wallace, James. *Overdrive: Bill Gates and the Race to Control Cyberspace.* New York: John Wiley & Sons, 1997.

Wallace, James, and Jim Erickson. *Hard Drive: Bill Gates and the Making of the Microsoft Empire.* New York: HarperBusiness, 1993.

—*Lisa Magloff*

Minimum Wage

The minimum wage is the lowest rate of pay for workers. A minimum wage can be set by federal legislation, unions, and associations. The federal minimum wage set by governments is most often used as a policy strategy to reduce poverty. In the United States, the Fair Labor Standards Act (FLSA) of 1938 was the first major piece of legislation adopted to set a minimum wage that applied to the entire nation. At that time, the law covered only 43 percent of all nonsupervisory wage and salary workers and was set at 25 cents per hour.

In 2003 the minimum wage was $5.15 an hour and covered about 90 percent of all nonsupervisory wage and salary workers. Workers not covered include those at small businesses that fall below the revenue threshold ($500,000 annual volume of business or less) addressed by the FLSA. More than 80 million American workers are covered by the FLSA, which is enforced by the Wage and Hour Division of the U.S. Department of Labor. The FLSA also sets rules prohibiting people under 18 years old from working in certain jobs and limits the hours and times that employees under 16 years of age may work.

Determining the proper level of the minimum wage is hotly debated among competing interests. Setting an effective minimum wage is based on a balance of two considerations. On the one hand, the higher the minimum wage rate, the higher the guaranteed income of workers, which helps reduce poverty. On the other, as the minimum wage is increased, employers have a harder time paying salaries and maintaining a profit and thus may be forced to stop hiring or even lay off existing workers because they are too costly.

See also:
Compensation; Fair Labor Standards Act; Great Depression; New Deal; Unemployment.

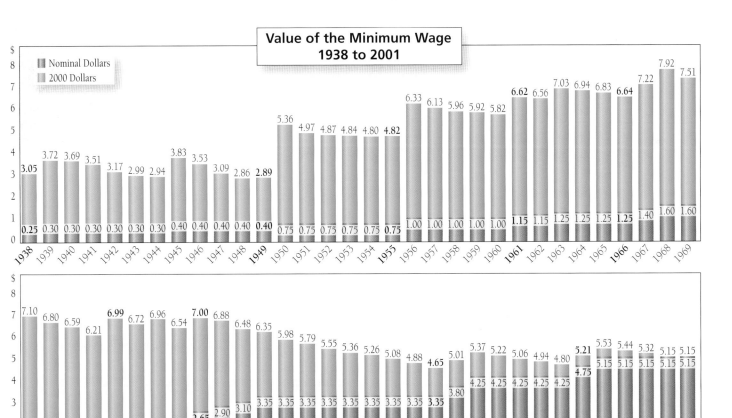

Value of the Minimum Wage 1938 to 2001

Note: **Bold** represents years in which the Fair Labor Standards Act was amended to raise the minimum wage.
Source: Bureau of Labor Statistics.

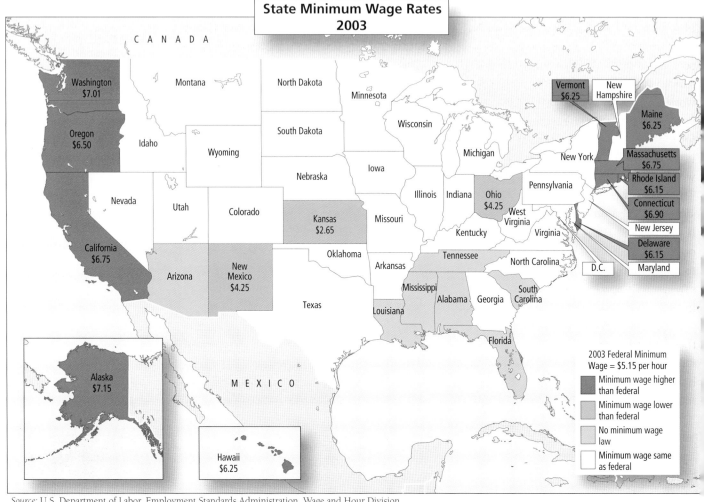

State Minimum Wage Rates 2003

CANADA

Washington
$7.01

Montana

North Dakota

Minnesota

Vermont
$6.25

New Hampshire

Maine
$6.25

Oregon
$6.50

Idaho

South Dakota

Wisconsin

Michigan

New York

Massachusetts
$6.75

Rhode Island
$6.15

Nevada

Wyoming

Nebraska

Iowa

Illinois

Indiana

Ohio
$4.25

Pennsylvania

Connecticut
$6.90

New Jersey

Utah

Colorado

Kansas
$2.65

Missouri

West Virginia

Virginia

Delaware
$6.15

California
$6.75

Arizona

New Mexico
$4.25

Oklahoma

Arkansas

Tennessee

Kentucky

North Carolina

D.C.

Maryland

Texas

Mississippi

Alabama

Georgia

South Carolina

Louisiana

Florida

2003 Federal Minimum
Wage = $5.15 per hour

Minimum wage higher than federal

Minimum wage lower than federal

No minimum wage law

Minimum wage same as federal

MEXICO

Alaska
$7.15

Hawaii
$6.25

Source: U.S. Department of Labor, Employment Standards Administration, Wage and Hour Division.

Many states have enacted legislation to set their own minimum wage higher than the national minimum wage.

Origins

The first national minimum wage law applying to all workers was enacted in New Zealand in 1894. In the United States, Massachusetts enacted the first minimum wage law in 1912. In the same year, eight other states also passed such laws. At that time, minimum wage legislation applied only to women and children. American labor unions opposed applying the minimum wage to men. Because unions helped their members bargain for higher wages with employers, the unions thought that the federal minimum wage would undermine the benefits they could provide to their members as the federal rate could supersede union-negotiated rates.

By 1923 minimum wage laws for women and minors were in place in 15 states, Puerto Rico, and the District of Columbia. However, that year a decision

of the U.S. Supreme Court eliminated all minimum wage laws on the basis that they were an unconstitutional government interference on private affairs.

In 1933, in response to the widespread economic hardships of the Great Depression, the Congress passed the National Industrial Recovery Act, which set minimum wage rates for both men and women. Two years later, however, the Supreme Court also declared this act unconstitutional.

The economic suffering of workers was a major campaign issue in the 1936 presidential race. The Democratic platform proposed to improve labor standards. Franklin D. Roosevelt campaigned on his New Deal vision, which promised to develop worker protection policies that could not be overturned by the Supreme Court. Roosevelt won the 1936 election by 523 electoral votes to 8 and interpreted his landslide victory as support for the New Deal.

On May 24, 1937, President Roosevelt sent a bill to Congress saying that America should be able to give "all our able-bodied working men and women a fair day's pay for a fair day's work." The initial proposal provided for a 40-cent-an-hour minimum wage, a 40-hour maximum workweek, and a minimum working age of 16 except in certain industries. The bill also proposed a five-member labor standards board, which could authorize still higher wages and shorter hours. Opponents of the bill said that it would lead the country to a "tyrannical industrial dictatorship." They saw the New Deal as a smoke screen disguising socialist planning.

Initially, unions opposed the bill because they feared that what was intended as a minimum wage might in the end become a maximum wage, and that wage boards would intervene in areas that unions wanted reserved for labor–management negotiations. Unions were satisfied when the bill was amended to exclude work covered by union negotiations.

On June 25, 1938, the president signed the FLSA to become effective on October 24, 1938. In the end, the minimum wage was set at 25 cents an hour.

Expansion of Coverage

When the national minimum wage was first established in the United States by the FLSA, it applied to only 43.4 percent of nonsupervisory employees and to those primarily employed in larger firms engaged in interstate commerce like manufacturing, mining, and construction companies.

In 1949 FLSA was expanded to include workers in the air transport industry. In 1961 amendments expanded the FLSA's scope in the retail trade sector for businesses with sales over $1 million, which

A demonstration calling for improved enforcement of the minimum wage law in Los Angeles, 1990.

extended coverage from 250,000 workers to 2.2 million. In 1966 coverage was further expanded to include retail businesses with sales of at least $500,000, starting in February 1967, and sales of at least $250,000 starting in February 1969. Also in 1966 changes were made to extend coverage to employees of public schools, nursing homes, laundries, and the entire construction industry. Farms were also subject to coverage for the first time.

In 1974 Congress made changes to include all nonsupervisory employees of federal, state, and local governments and many domestic workers. In 1981 the $250,000 threshold for retail trade and service enterprises was increased in stages to $362,500 to adjust for inflation.

Currently, an employee can be covered by the law in two ways: "enterprise coverage" and "individual coverage." Employees are covered if they work in enterprises that earn at least $500,000 a year in business or are hospitals, businesses providing medical or nursing care for residents, schools and preschools, and government agencies. Employees are also protected by the FLSA if their work regularly involves them in commerce between states.

Economics and Politics

The debates over whether to have a minimum wage or how much to increase the minimum wage focus on the base salary needed to make a living versus whether people will lose their jobs as a result of a higher minimum wage. Advocates on both sides of the argument—politicians, special interest groups, and activists—can find support from economists.

As employers are forced to pay their workers higher wages, their costs increase and profits shrink. At some point, if the minimum wage continues to increase, employers could be forced to avoid hiring new workers or even lay off workers to pay the higher wages. Some economists argue that workers themselves should determine the lowest wage that they are willing to work for, not the government. This reasoning is based on the idea that a worker will not accept a job unless it pays enough to support him. Setting a rate higher than this by imposing a minimum wage, they argue,

In a 1996 ceremony on the White House lawn, President Bill Clinton signed a bill raising the minimum wage. He is joined by Vice President Al Gore and the children of those earning minimum wage.

is artificial interference in the market, which prevents those who are willing to work for less from accepting certain jobs.

Other economists argue that if a minimum wage is not set, employers will exploit the poor by paying them less than they can live on, even though the employers would be able to pay more. They also argue that basic fairness requires that people who work full-time should earn enough to support themselves and their families.

Another important consideration is inflation, which erodes the purchasing power of the minimum wage. As the cost of goods rises, a person earning the minimum wage is able to buy less. Thus, advocates for increasing the minimum wage often point out that the value of the minimum wage is effectively lower than it used to be, because it is able to buy fewer goods. Thus, to maintain the basic living standards of minimum-wage earners, the rate must be increased.

Experts agree that there is always some level of the minimum wage that will be too high, such that some workers will lose their jobs. Disagreements arise around defining that figure. Most studies indicate that the recent small increases in the minimum wage cause no or minimal job loss. Some economists think that increasing the minimum wage could increase employment because, by paying more for their time, such increase would provide a stronger reason for those who are not working at all to get a job.

Employers in industries that rely heavily on low-wage workers, including small-business owners, retail stores, and restaurants, typically are the most vocal opponents of increasing the minimum wage. Meanwhile, unions are typically the most vocal supporters of minimum wage increases.

The minimum wage is usually seen as one part of a multifaceted approach to alleviating poverty. The most significant parallel policy is the Earned Income Tax Credit (EITC), which provides tax credits to working people in an effort to increase their income. As a result of the combined effects of the minimum wage and the EITC, a family with a single full-time minimum-wage

Hourly Workers with Earnings at or below the Federal Minimum Wage 2001	Number (in thousands)	Percent*
Sex and Age		
16 to 24 years	1,206	7.3
25 years and over	1,032	1.8
Total	2,238	3.1
Men		
16 to 24 years	473	5.6
25 years and over	311	1.1
Total	784	2.2
Women		
16 to 24 years	733	9.0
25 years and over	721	2.5
Total	1,454	4.0
Race and Hispanic Origin by Sex		
White		
Men	641	2.2
Women	1,219	4.2
Total	1,861	3.1
Black		
Men	114	2.5
Women	183	3.4
Total	297	3.0
Hispanic origin		
Men	138	2.4
Women	164	3.8
Total	302	3.0
Full- and Part-time Workers by Sex		
Full-time workers		
Men	328	1.1
Women	525	2.1
Total	853	1.5
Part-time workers		
Men	455	8.3
Women	923	7.9
Total	1,378	8.0

*Percent of total number of hourly workers within category by age, sex, race, and so forth.
Source: Bureau of Labor Statistics, http://www.bls.gov/cps/cpsaat44.pdf (February 21, 2003).

worker and one or two children can now earn enough money to avoid poverty.

Raising the Minimum Wage
The first minimum wage was less than half (40 percent) of the average wage for manufacturing workers. This does not reflect the purchasing power of the minimum wage in

Current and Real Values of the Minimum Wage 1960 to 2001

Current dollar
Real (1999) dollar

Source: Economic Policy Institute, *The State of Working America, 2000–01,* Economic Policy Institute, Washington, D.C., fig 2T, and U.S. Department of Labor, *Value of the Federal Minimum Wage, 1954–1996.*

current dollars, because over the years inflation erodes the real value. The original rate is called the nominal rate, and the rate adjusting for inflation is called the real rate. If one were to recalculate 25 cents in current purchasing power by adjusting for inflation, in 2000 this rate would have been equivalent to $3.05.

The minimum wage rate does not increase automatically. Unlike many industrialized nations, the United States has no technical formula to determine periodic, automatic cost-of-living increases in the minimum wage. Rather, Congress must pass a bill that the president signs into law for the minimum wage to be increased.

By 2002 the minimum wage had been increased eight times by legislation. The purchasing power of the minimum wage reached a peak in 1970, when it was set at $2.65, equivalent to $7.00 in 2000 dollars. The minimum wage bill passed in 1996

increased the minimum wage to $4.75 an hour on October 1, 1996, and to $5.15 an hour on September 1, 1997. About 10 million workers benefited from this increase. Approximately 70 percent were adults (20 years or older), 58 percent were women, and 33 percent were black or Hispanic. Almost half (46 percent) worked full-time. In 1997 the earnings of the average minimum-wage worker accounted for 54 percent of his or her family's total earnings.

Further Reading

Ehrenberg, Ronald, and Robert S. Smith. *Modern Labor Economics: Theory and Public Policy.* 7th ed. Reading, Mass.: Addison Wesley, 2000.

Stiglitz, Joseph E. *Economics.* 3rd ed. New York: Norton, 2002.

U.S. Department of Labor. *Minimum Wage and Maximum Hours Standards under the Fair Labor Standards Act, 1988.* Report to the Congress under Section 4(d)(1) of the FLSA.

—*Carl Haack*

Mining Industry

Mining has an ancient lineage. Large-scale mining dates to the ancient Egyptians who quarried obelisks out of rock using wooden wedges driven into channels dug into the rock and then doused with water until they swelled enough to break out a section of rock. The technology of mining has since improved enormously, especially in wealthy countries.

In some ways, however, the mining industry has changed little: mining remains an extractive industry, focused on exploiting valuable minerals usually found in underground deposits. Mining companies cannot freely choose where to operate; they must dig where the deposits are. Although the technology used has changed immensely, the basic industry cycle of discovery, exploitation, and exhaustion of deposits has not greatly altered since the days when the pharaohs ruled Egypt.

A remarkable array of substances with vastly different uses are mined. Precious metals, including gold and platinum (which also have industrial uses), and gemstones like diamonds are mined. Metals used widely in construction, like iron and aluminum, are mined, as are lead, copper, and zinc. However, metals make up only about a quarter of the value of mined substances. The so-called energy minerals—petroleum, coal, and gas—are also mined. Other mined nonmetals include phosphate and potash (used in fertilizer), sulfur, salt, and gypsum.

In most countries, including the United States, mining is not a very large industry. Mining employs only slightly more than half a million people in the United States, a small share of the overall workforce. However, the minerals produced by mining are vital to a wide array of industries, as well as to agriculture. In the United States, the estimate is that every $1 of mineral production supports $10 of industrial production.

See also:
Environmental Regulation;
Organization of Petroleum
Exporting Countries; Royal
Dutch/Shell; Texaco;
Working Conditions.

A coal mine, circa 1920s.

A miner looks up the shaft of a drill in an underground mine in Wallace, Idaho.

No one country has reserves of all the minerals needed by industry and agriculture. The United States, for example, is a major producer of coal, phosphate, aluminum, and other important substances. Nonetheless, the United States is largely dependent on imports for petroleum, bauxite, cobalt, chromium, and many other essential materials.

Mineral deposits are often located far from the industries that use them and are sometimes in places that are very inconvenient for other reasons. For example, consider high-tech tools like laptop computers, handheld digital assistants, and cellular phones. Some of their electronic components are made of tantalum, a heat-resistant metal that conducts electricity very well. Tantalum is made from coltan, which is found in abundance in wilderness preserves in the eastern region of the war-torn and impoverished Democratic Republic of the Congo. Not only are the deposits far from the U.S.–based makers of tantalum components, but high prices for coltan in the late 1990s sparked a mining frenzy in the eastern Congo, worsening local conflicts and

destroying delicate ecosystems, until eventually makers of tantalum components pledged to stop using Congolese coltan.

The United States has become more and more reliant on mineral imports in recent decades, despite occasional campaigns by policy makers to more fully exploit domestic mineral resources. Indeed, the value of minerals imported into the United States began to outpace the value of exports in the 1940s.

Challenges of the Mining Industry

Several factors have driven up the cost of mining in the United States, making imports relatively cheap. The country has been relatively well explored by prospectors over the past couple of centuries, and most of the readily accessible deposits of ore with a high mineral content were found long ago. Another factor is the relatively high wage scale in the United States.

Still another is the cost of environmental regulation. Mining is notoriously damaging to the environment; some streams in the Rocky Mountains are still polluted from nineteenth-century mining activity. The least expensive way to mine a deposit is by open-pit mining—the top layers of soil are stripped off by machinery or blown away with explosives. This method is extremely destructive to the plants and animals that were living atop that soil.

Open-pit mining can also radically change the wider landscape. Digs leave massive craters, and sometimes the tops are taken off hills to reach valuable deposits. Mining companies in the United States do attempt to rehabilitate areas, trucking in topsoil and planting new vegetation. Yet only about half of the land used for mining in recent decades has ever been rehabilitated, and critics charge that the damage to the landscape and environment caused by open-pit mining is not remediable.

Even underground mining, where tunnels are dug down to the deposit, can have a severe environmental impact. Such tunnels are designed to lead to mineral-rich ores, but many minerals are toxic in high concentrations

Water can enter the tunnels, leach out the toxic minerals, and then poison wildlife or contaminate drinking water.

The effect of mining on the environment and the landscape is especially galling to critics of the industry because mines are usually short-term operations that provide only limited economic benefits to an area. Once a deposit is identified and mining begins, the deposit will eventually be fully exploited and the mine shut down. Some deposits are so vast that they can support decades of mining, but many are small and are used up in only a few years, or they are expensive to exploit because the ore does not contain much mineral or the deposit is extremely deep, so the mines operate only when the price of that mineral is very high.

Consequently resentment of the mining industry runs high in many countries, and the industry is heavily regulated worldwide. Indeed, during the 1960s and 1970s, many countries nationalized large mines and large mining operations, putting them under direct government control. Nationalization was seen as a way to ensure that the mining industry served the public interest; in poorer countries, nationalization was seen as a way to avoid exploitation by foreign-owned mining firms.

Pricing Minerals

State ownership of mines has contributed to a problem that plagues the industry—the prices of many minerals tend to fall partly because minerals are a commodity that tend to compete solely on price—bauxite is bauxite, wherever it comes from. In some cases, cartels have been established to restrain supply and keep prices relatively

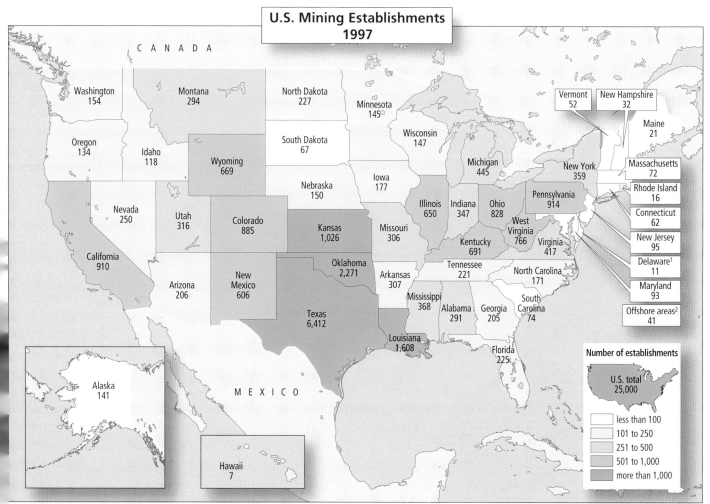

U.S. Mining Establishments 1997

Washington 154
Montana 294
North Dakota 227
Minnesota 145
Oregon 134
Idaho 118
Wyoming 669
South Dakota 67
Wisconsin 147
Michigan 445
Vermont 52
New Hampshire 32
Maine 21
New York 359
Massachusetts 72
Nevada 250
Utah 316
Colorado 885
Nebraska 150
Iowa 177
Illinois 650
Indiana 347
Ohio 828
Pennsylvania 914
Rhode Island 16
Connecticut 62
California 910
Kansas 1,026
Missouri 306
Kentucky 691
West Virginia 766
Virginia 417
New Jersey 95
Delaware[1] 11
Arizona 206
New Mexico 606
Oklahoma 2,271
Arkansas 307
Tennessee 221
North Carolina 171
Maryland 93
Offshore areas[2] 41
Texas 6,412
Mississippi 368
Alabama 291
Georgia 205
South Carolina 74
Louisiana 1,608
Florida 225
Alaska 141
Hawaii 7

CANADA
MEXICO

Number of establishments

U.S. total 25,000

less than 100
101 to 250
251 to 500
501 to 1,000
more than 1,000

[1] District of Columbia is included with Delaware. [2] Not associated with a state.
Source: U.S. Bureau of the Census, *1997 Economic Census, Mining, Series EC97N21S-GS,* Washington, D.C., Government Printing Office, 2001.

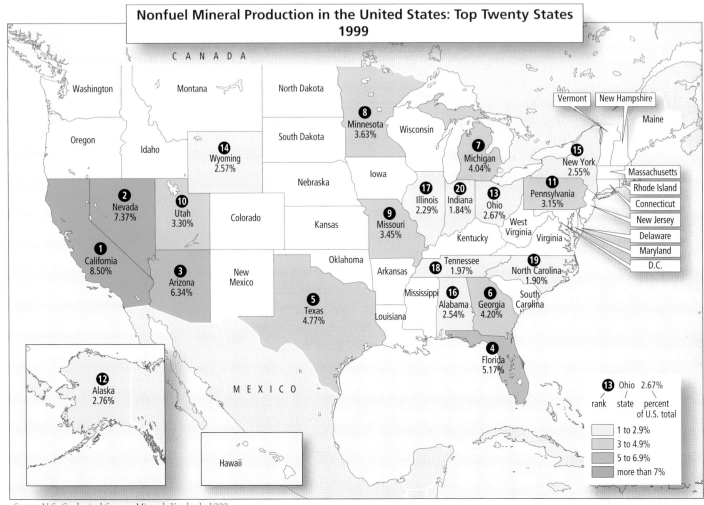

Nonfuel Mineral Production in the United States: Top Twenty States 1999

Washington

Oregon

Idaho

Nevada
7.37% ❷

California
8.50% ❶

Arizona
6.34% ❸

Utah
3.30% ❿

Wyoming
2.57% ⓮

Montana

North Dakota

South Dakota

Nebraska

Colorado

Kansas

New Mexico

Texas
4.77% ❺

CANADA

Minnesota
3.63% ❽

Wisconsin

Iowa

Missouri
3.45% ❾

Oklahoma

Arkansas

Mississippi

Louisiana

Michigan
4.04% ❼

Illinois
2.29% ⓱

Indiana
1.84% ⓴

Ohio
2.67% ⓭

Kentucky

West Virginia

Tennessee
1.97% ⓲

Alabama
2.54% ⓰

Georgia
4.20% ❻

New York
2.55% ⓯

Pennsylvania
3.15% ⑪

Virginia

North Carolina
1.90% ⑲

South Carolina

Florida
5.17% ❹

Vermont | New Hampshire

Maine

Massachusetts
Rhode Island
Connecticut
New Jersey
Delaware
Maryland
D.C.

Alaska
2.76% ⓬

MEXICO

Hawaii

❭ Ohio 2.67%
rank state percent
of U.S. total

1 to 2.9%
3 to 4.9%
5 to 6.9%
more than 7%

Source: U.S. Geological Survey, *Minerals Yearbook*, 1999.

high, most notably the Organization of Petroleum Exporting Countries (OPEC) and the DeBeers diamond cartel. In many other cases, forming cartels has proven to be impossible. Many state-owned mining firms produce the greatest possible amount no matter what the market because exports of minerals are an important source of foreign currency for many governments and because such firms often have a mandate to keep unemployment as low as possible.

Why are prices falling for minerals? Minerals are a nonrenewable resource—once they are gone, they are gone forever—and the world's population keeps increasing. However, a number of factors have kept prices down.

The technology used to make discoveries and exploit deposits has improved dramatically. Although mining geologists still use older discovery techniques like

exploring upstream from a riverbed where chunks of minerals have been found, they also have an array of sophisticated devices to help them find underground deposits. These devices can detect minor variations in magnetism and density, satellites take infrared photographs, and powerful computers create models pinpointing likely spots to dig or drill. Improvements in extraction technology make it possible to restore to productivity old mines that were once thought to be tapped out.

Such technology has made mining even more capital intensive than before. Simply discovering a deposit and attempting to determine its value can cost tens of millions of dollars, but because actually building a mine costs even more, the price of exploration is considered worthwhile. As a result, the mining industry is dominated in wealthy countries by large multinational

Mine blasting in Colorado.

corporations that can afford to conduct large-scale exploration and mining.

Another reason mineral prices have not increased is that industries are always looking for substitutes for expensive and rare minerals that might not always be reliably supplied. Bauxite was once essential to the production of aluminum; now certain clays are used. Likewise, telephone lines that were once exclusively made of copper are now made of glass fiber-optic cable as well. High prices for virgin material encourage the recycling of reusable metals like aluminum and iron.

In addition, the transition of the economies of the world's wealthiest countries from industrial economies to service economies has dampened overall demand for the products of the mining industry. World demand for metals continues to rise but at a much slower rate since the mid-1960s.

Nonetheless, mining has a future; the use of information technology in recent years is what created fierce demand for tantalum. Although mining may become an ever-smaller part of the world economy, it is likely that it will always be a critical component of the industrial and post-industrial world.

Further Reading

Brooks, David B., ed. *Resource Economics: Selected Works of Orris C. Herfindahl.* Washington, D.C.: Resources for the Future, 1974.

Mikesell, Raymond F., and John W. Whitney. *The World Mining Industry: Investment Strategy and Public Policy.* Boston: Allen & Unwin, 1987.

Taylor, Alex, II. "Oil Oil Everywhere." *Fortune,* 16 April 2001, 148.

Van Rensburg, W. C. J. *Strategic Minerals.* 2 vols. Englewood Cliffs, N.J.: Prentice-Hall, 1986.

—*Mary Sisson*

Careers in the Mining Industry

The mining industry hardly has the most appealing history for workers. From enslaved salt miners in North Africa to U.S. coal workers dying from black-lung disease, the history of mining labor is one of danger, disease, and impoverishment.

However, technology has radically changed mining work in the United States. Safety in mines has been dramatically improved because of newer methods to guard against cave-ins and explosions, as well as tough federal safety regulations. Fatalities in mining have fallen from 3,197 in 1907, to 342 in 1971, to 156 in 2000.

Where miners used to dig, they now operate heavy equipment that does the digging, and some specialize in explosives. Mining work pays relatively well, but because old mines become depleted and new mines in other locations replace them, miners tend to move around a lot. Some miners, like workers on offshore oil rigs, are isolated from their families for long periods.

The mining industry employs more than miners. Modern methods of exploration require geologists who can use a wide variety of technical tools to evaluate potential mining sites, as well as computer experts and others who can support that technology. Some mining companies have even hired botanists to analyze the growth of surface plants to see if they show signs that the soil is rich in a particular mineral.

See also:

Arts and Entertainment Industry; Screen Actors Guild; Walt Disney Company.

Miramax Films

In the 1980s filmmakers in Hollywood focused on producing popular, big-budget, blockbuster films. Independent filmmakers had difficulty finding a studio that would pay for the creation and release of small-scale, offbeat films or films made by young filmmakers. The decades since have seen many changes, with no studio, distributor, or production company having done more to build a mainstream audience for independent and foreign films than Miramax.

Miramax was founded in 1979 by Bob and Harvey Weinstein, who named the company after their parents, Miriam and Max. They sought to create a home for films not deemed commercially viable by major Hollywood studios. A trip to the Cannes Film Festival in 1979 helped the Weinsteins get started. At Cannes they purchased distribution rights to *The Secret Policeman's Ball*—a film documentary of a charity rock concert too obscure for the major studios to touch—for $180,000. In part because of the Weinsteins' marketing guidance, the film grossed $6 million, which became the seed money for Miramax.

Miramax succeeded by developing marketing strategies that brought challenging, controversial films to the attention of average filmgoers, thereby increasing the audience for small films. One strategy was to generate publicity by creating controversy. In 1990, for example, Miramax distributed a film about gay drag balls in Harlem, *Paris Is Burning*, and a satirical farce, *The Pope Must Die,* both of which were condemned by religious organizations. The resulting publicity helped make the formerly obscure films into box-office

Miramax Films

1979
Miramax founded by Bob and Harvey Weinstein.

1990
Miramax sues MPAA over X rating of two films.

1989
Miramax wins first Oscar for *My Left Foot*.

1993
Disney buys Miramax for $75 million.

1998
Miramax garners 23 Oscar nominations.

2001
Miramax becomes first major studio to distribute a feature film, *Guinevere*, over the Internet.

successes. The high quality of mos Miramax films also increased their popu larity. Miramax won its first Oscar for M Left Foot (1989); between 1989 and 2000 Miramax films received 148 Oscar nomina tions and won 42 Oscars.

Sometimes Miramax's marketing strate gies also involved picking fights with th Motion Picture Association of Americ (MPAA). In 1990 two films distributed b Miramax, *Tie Me Up! Tie Me Down!* and *Th Cook, the Thief, His Wife and Her Love* received X ratings from the MPAA, which i considered to be a death blow to any film because most theaters will not show X-rate films. Miramax sued the MPAA. The case wa dismissed, but the publicity guaranteed th success of both films and it also forced th MPAA to create a new rating, NC-17.

In 1993 the film industry was shocke when the kid-friendly Disney Compan purchased the controversial Miramax fc

The journey is outrageous, and maintaining it is fun, too. Don't get me wrong, having money and success is great, but you know what? The journey up is a riot—if you have good friends, nerves of steel and tenacity. Never take no for an answer, and if anyone tells you no to get you off your course or off your game, don't believe that for a second. There are no rules.

— Harvey Weinstein, interview with *The Guardian,* September 28, 2001

an estimated $75 million. The contract with Disney left the Weinsteins in charge of Miramax, and the money allowed Miramax to expand the movie production portion of its business.

A string of hits followed, including *Muriel's Wedding* (1994) and *Pulp Fiction* (1994); the latter cost $8 million to make and grossed over $200 million. Through a savvy marketing campaign that involved phoning members of the Motion Picture Academy directly to ask for their vote, Miramax garnered several 1995 Oscar nominations for *Il Postino* (*The Postman*, 1994). In 1996 Miramax distributed *The English Patient*, which won five Oscars, including best picture. It also purchased the Japanese film *Shall We Dance?* for $300,000, earning $9.5 million on it. In 1998 Miramax garnered 23 Oscar nominations, including two for best picture: *Life Is Beautiful* and *Shakespeare in Love*, which won the award.

Like the Hollywood studios of the 1930s, Miramax also runs a genre film subsidiary—Dimension Films. Run by Bob Weinstein, Dimension Films is responsible for science fiction and horror films. Dimension's films rarely win Oscars, but they earn considerably more money than the Miramax releases.

In 2001 Miramax Films became the first major movie studio to send a feature film over the Internet, with the digital delivery of *Guinevere*, a romance film originally released in 1999. Users could download the film and use it for 24 hours, after first buying a license for $3.49.

All this success has made Hollywood moguls of the Weinsteins. Harvey is the public face of Miramax, epitomizing the company's street-smart New York roots and earning the nickname "Harvey Scissorhands" for his propensity to bully filmmakers in the cutting room. Bob is known as "Mr. Inside" for his quieter handling of finances. Even by Hollywood standards, the brothers are said to be arrogant. *Variety* magazine has reported that Harvey once locked a producer in a hotel room until the

Miramax cofounder Harvey Weinstein at the Venice Film Festival in 1999.

producer agreed to sell Miramax the rights to distribute his film. In 1993 *Fortune* magazine named the Weinsteins among the 70 toughest bosses in America.

However, no one questions the Weinsteins' dedication to getting independent, foreign, and low-budget movies into mainstream theaters. Their efforts have helped to revitalize the movie industry and have inspired numerous imitators. In an expression of the sincerest form of flattery, Sony, Fox, and Universal have now launched their own art-house subsidiary studios to compete with Miramax.

Further Reading

Abramowitz, Rachel. *Is That a Gun in Your Pocket?: Women's Experience of Power in Hollywood.* New York: Random House, 2000.

Greene, Ray. *Hollywood Migraine: The Inside Story of a Decade in Film.* Dublin: Merlin Publishing, 2001.

Rosenbaum, Jonathan. *Movie Wars: How Hollywood and the Media Conspire to Limit the Films We See.* Chicago: A Cappella Books, 2000.

—Lisa Magloff

See also:
Globalization;
Manufacturing Industry;
Transportation Industry.

Mitsubishi Motors

Mitsubishi is a familiar name to most Americans, largely because Mitsubishi Motors Corporation is Japan's fourth-largest automaker. Mitsubishi is not a single company, however. It is a businesses entity known in Japan as a *keiretsu*. A *keiretsu* is a group of companies that own shares in one another and support one another in business. Mitsubishi is the largest *keiretsu* in Japan, encompassing hundreds of companies that generate some $300 billion in annual revenues.

Capitalism in Japan has developed in ways that differ somewhat from the form it has taken in the United States; Mitsubishi's history reflects that development. Mitsubishi was founded in the 1870s by Iwasaki Yataro, the son of a samurai family that had fallen on hard times and lost its title. Although Iwasaki was excluded from Japan's more prestigious schools, he possessed intelligence and drive—enough so that he eventually was put in charge of a trading office in Osaka established by the government of his home region. In 1870 the reformist Meiji government of Japan decided to strip the regional governments of many of their powers. The trading office where Iwasaki worked was privatized, and he was placed in control of the new company. Three years later, Iwasaki named the company Mitsubishi, or "three diamonds," a reference to the company's logo, which was adopted from the Iwasaki family crest.

Under Iwasaki's leadership, Mitsubishi entered the shipping business. This was a patriotic gesture as well as a shrewd business move; until this point the only shipping companies in Japan with large, modern ships were American or European. The Meiji government supported Mitsubishi, fearing that foreigners would come to dominate Japan's economy if they controlled long-distance shipping, a crucial industry for an island nation. In return, Mitsubishi's ships were

Mitsubishi's Kobe plant, circa 1925.

always available to transport government soldiers and munitions.

By the 1880s Mitsubishi had dozens of ships and a monopoly on the long-distance shipping business. Mitsubishi's power was resented, however, and the company was dubbed "the Sea Goblin" by critics. In 1885 the government effectively forced Mitsubishi out of the shipping business. That year, Iwasaki Yataro died, and his brother, Iwasaki Yanosuke, became president of the company.

With Mitsubishi unable to remain in shipping, Iwasaki Yanosuke pursued a strategy called "from the sea to the land," developing businesses like coal mining, shipbuilding, warehousing, trading, and insurance that Mitsubishi had initially entered to support the shipping business. Iwasaki Yanosuke also made sure to keep Mitsubishi a family business, grooming Iwasaki Yataro's son Iwasaki Hisaya and his own son Iwasaki Koyata to run the company.

Mitsubishi's businesses eventually expanded to include steel, banking, automobiles, and airplanes. After Iwasaki Koyata became president in 1916, he began spinning off Mitsubishi's various businesses into separate companies. Despite being separate, all the companies were tightly controlled by a holding company owned primarily by the Iwasaki family—an arrangement known as a *zaibatsu*. By 1930 the Iwasakis controlled the second-largest *zaibatsu* in Japan, with more than 60 companies concentrated in heavy industry.

The *zaibatsu* system soon came to an end for Mitsubishi. During the 1930s Japan's government became increasingly fascistic and its military increasingly aggressive. In December 1941 Japanese forces attacked a U.S. Navy base at Pearl Harbor, Hawaii, drawing the United States into World War II. Because of its focus on heavy industry, the Mitsubishi *zaibatsu* was deeply involved with Japan's war effort, manufacturing armaments like the Zero fighter plane. Despite Iwasaki Koyata's lukewarm support for the war—he refused to allow Mitsubishi executives to advise the government—Japan's military was so dependent

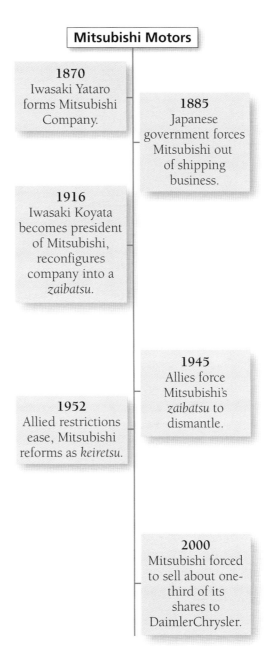

Mitsubishi Motors

1870
Iwasaki Yataro forms Mitsubishi Company.

1885
Japanese government forces Mitsubishi out of shipping business.

1916
Iwasaki Koyata becomes president of Mitsubishi, reconfigures company into a *zaibatsu*.

1945
Allies force Mitsubishi's *zaibatsu* to dismantle.

1952
Allied restrictions ease, Mitsubishi reforms as *keiretsu*.

2000
Mitsubishi forced to sell about one-third of its shares to DaimlerChrysler.

on Mitsubishi products that it was sometimes called the Mitsubishi Arsenal.

When Japan surrendered to the U.S.–backed Allied forces in 1945, a primary goal of the Allies was to dismantle Japan's war machine, which meant dismantling the *zaibatsu*. The Mitsubishi holding company was dissolved, as were several of the larger Mitsubishi companies. The Mitsubishi name was banned, and members of the Iwasaki family were forced to resign and give up their holdings in the companies.

By the 1950s, however, the tight controls on the former *zaibatsu* began to ease. In 1952 companies could again use the Mitsubishi name, and many former Mitsubishi

The Mitsubishi Space Liner on display at the Paris Auto Show in September 2002.

companies reclaimed their old names. Restrictions designed to prevent the *zaibatsu* companies from joining forces were also eased, and Mitsubishi companies began to reconnect. Nonetheless, the *zaibatsu* era, with its family control and highly centralized command structure, did not survive. Instead, the companies formed a looser alliance, a *keiretsu*. The larger companies of the *keiretsu* provided general strategic leadership, and the various Mitsubishi companies tried to help each other.

In the 1960s the Mitsubishi *keiretsu* began to move into international markets. By 1971 the Mitsubishi *keiretsu* decided that it not only needed to sell worldwide—it also needed to develop global businesses. By the end of the 1980s many Mitsubishi companies were global players with factories worldwide. As Mitsubishi companies expanded, their membership in the *keiretsu* gave them many advantages. Mitsubishi's bank, for example, could give other Mitsubishi companies access to cheap capital. Mitsubishi companies that sold finished goods could give preferential treatment to Mitsubishi suppliers; the suppliers could return the favor.

In the early 1990s, however, Japan entered a period of economic weakness from which it has yet to recover, and the drawbacks of the *keiretsu* system became abundantly clear. Loans from profitable companies within the *keiretsu* had been used to prop up unprofitable firms that probably should have been restructured or allowed to go out of business. The result was financial weakness throughout the entire *keiretsu*.

The centralized leadership of the Mitsubishi *keiretsu* has also hampered globalization. Although Mitsubishi's companies have facilities overseas, top foreign talent is often hard to attract because the important decisions are made by a handful of executives, who can be insensitive to local concerns in Tokyo. By 2000 Mitsubishi's largest companies were eking out puny returns or losing money. Mitsubishi Motors—further damaged by revelations that the company had been concealing defects in its cars since the 1980s—was forced to sell roughly one-third of its shares to DaimlerChrysler, which eventually took over management of the carmaker. Like Japan as a whole, Mitsubishi at the turn of the twenty-first century faced an uncertain future likely to entail either continued poor economic performance or painful structural reform.

Further Reading

Mishima, Yasuo. *The Mitsubishi: Its Challenge and Strategy.* Translated by Emiko Yamaguchi. Greenwich, Conn.: JAI Press, 1989.

Rudlin, Pernille. *The History of the Mitsubishi Corporation in London: 1915 to Present Day.* London: Routledge, 2000.

Wray, William D. *Mitsubishi and the N.Y.K., 1870–1914: Business Strategy in the Japanese Shipping Industry.* Cambridge, Mass.: Harvard University Press, 1984.

—*Mary Sisson*

Monetary Policy

Monetary policy controls a country's money supply, which in turn determines how much an economy can expand or contract. By manipulating the total amount of money available, a country's central bank (in the United States, the Federal Reserve) can influence monetary and credit conditions to promote employment, economic growth, and low inflation. The Federal Reserve (also known as the Fed) typically seeks to control the supply of money and the level of key short-term interest rates as means of implementing its policy.

The Objectives of Monetary Policy

The U.S. government is required by the Employment Act of 1946 (which was later reaffirmed in the Full Employment and Balanced Growth Act of 1978) to aim for high employment and stable prices. As a government agency, the Fed must pursue a policy course consistent with achieving these objectives. As evidence suggests that monetary and credit conditions are statistically linked to employment, output, and inflation, the Fed must control money growth or the level of short-term interest rates to meet these objectives.

Observers sometimes disagree about the extent to which monetary policy objectives are consistent with one another. For example, some researchers argue that efforts to lower unemployment and stimulate growth of output can be inflationary, thereby interfering with Fed attempts to deliver price stability. Still others argue that monetary policies that prove inflationary can lead to inefficiencies in the use of economic resources and can cause output to grow less rapidly in the long run. Uncertainties about the economic effects of monetary policy can markedly complicate the decisions of the Fed.

Evidence suggests that in the short run (probably as long as 18 months), monetary policy can and does influence employment and output growth. To see how this might happen, imagine that the Fed has decided to make credit more plentiful by expanding the supply of money. Increased availability of credit tends to make the cost of obtaining credit (the interest rate) decline. These lower rates make financing the construction of new homes less costly; businesses can also invest in new equipment, machinery, and structures at a lower cost. Consumers also find purchasing new motor vehicles, furniture, and appliances less expensive. These greater expenditures lead to more output. With more spending on new output, firms must hire more people to achieve production goals. Thus, employment increases and unemployment falls when the Fed increases credit availability. The opposite can be expected to occur when the Fed tightens monetary policy.

The Tools of Monetary Policy

The Fed uses three tools to influence the money supply and short-term interest rates: open market operations, discount policy, and reserve requirements. Before these tools can be explained, understanding the role of bank reserves in the implementation of monetary policy is crucial. Banks hold reserves as cash in vaults or as deposits that they maintain at a regional Federal Reserve bank. When reserves in the banking system become more plentiful, the federal funds rate decreases; the federal funds rate is the rate that banks charge one another for the overnight use of reserves (this interest rate is unfortunately named as there is really nothing "federal" about this market-determined rate). The federal funds rate has played a key role in Federal Reserve monetary policy operations in recent years. When newspapers report that the Fed has lowered interest rates, what they are actually reporting is that the central bank's target for the federal funds rate has

See also:
Economic Growth; Federal Reserve System; Fiscal Policy; Greenspan, Alan; Inflation.

Tools of Monetary Policy	
Required reserves	Portion of funds a depository institution is required to maintain as vault cash or on deposit with a Federal Reserve Bank
Discount rate	Rate of interest the Fed charges on loans to member banks
Open market operations	The Fed's purchase and sale of previously issued U.S. government securities

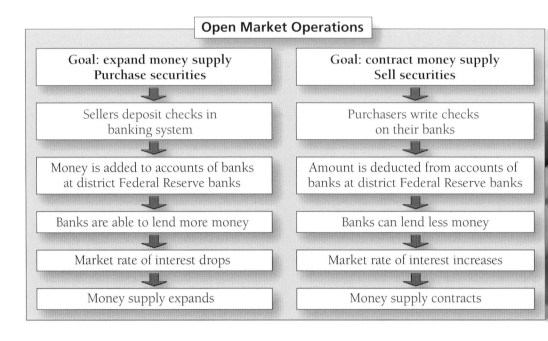

Open Market Operations

Goal: expand money supply Purchase securities	Goal: contract money supply Sell securities
Sellers deposit checks in banking system	Purchasers write checks on their banks
Money is added to accounts of banks at district Federal Reserve banks	Amount is deducted from accounts of banks at district Federal Reserve banks
Banks are able to lend more money	Banks can lend less money
Market rate of interest drops	Market rate of interest increases
Money supply expands	Money supply contracts

been lowered. When the Fed wishes to ease monetary policy, it uses its tools to increase the supply of reserves in the banking system and reduce the cost of obtaining these reserves (which is the federal funds rate). A reduction in bank reserves has the opposite effect, causing the federal funds rate to rise.

Open market operations are the buying and selling of existing government securities by the Federal Reserve. When the Fed arranges to purchase existing Treasury bonds, notes, or bills, the supply of reserves in the banking system increases and the federal

funds rate falls. Open market operations are easily the most frequently used tool of monetary policy. For example, if the Fed wishes to pursue a more expansionary monetary policy, it will lower the federal funds rate target and take a more aggressive approach to the buying of existing government securities. This will naturally cause the supply of reserves in the banking system to rise and will likely stimulate short-term economic activity. Again, this also works in the reverse: determination to tighten the availability of credit will typically involve the selling of existing government securities (otherwise known as open market sales), leading to a reduction in the supply of bank reserves and an increase in the federal funds rate.

The second most frequently used monetary policy tool is discount policy. The discount rate is the rate the Fed charges banks that borrow reserves (in the form of discount loans) from Federal Reserve banks. This rate is set by Fed policy makers and is not market determined. Banks are typically discouraged from using discount loans because the Fed expects banks to use market sources of funds to meet their short-term need for reserves. Banks that "overuse" the discount facility are likely to attract Fed scrutiny. Perhaps the most important function of discount policy is that it allows the Fed to provide liquidity to financial markets during times of heightened

Aggregrate Reserves of Depository Institutions 2002
(in million dollars)

Date	Total	Required
January	43,698	42,303
February	42,472	41,101
March	40,302	38,881
April	40,893	39,682
May	40,225	38,964
June	38,540	37,301
July	39,317	37,943
August	39,741	38,104
September	38,781	37,305
October	38,542	36,992
November	38,982	37,366
December	40,045	38,061

Source: Federal Reserve Board, "Aggregate Reserves of Depository Institutions and the Monetary Base," http://www.federalreserve.gov/release/h3/ (January 9, 2003).

uncertainty. For example, in the days following the September 11, 2001, terrorist attacks, the Fed supplied $45 billion of discount loans to the banking system. This represented an almost unimaginable 76,000 percent increase in the level of discount loans from the ordinary level of $59 million in the weeks before the terrorist attacks. When the banking system has no other immediate source of funds, the Federal Reserve can use its discount facilities to make funds available to banks. This allows the Fed to promote economic stability by serving as lender of last resort.

The Fed is usually very reluctant to change reserve requirements, the third tool of monetary policy. Banks do not keep all the money deposited with them immediately on hand; much of the money saved in banks is, in fact, invested or lent out to others.

However, all U.S. depository institutions are required to maintain a fraction of depositors' checking accounts in the form of reserves. This fraction was one-tenth, or 10 percent, at the end of 2001. This fraction, known as the required reserve ratio, had not been changed since April 1992. To illustrate how reserve requirements are tabulated, imagine a bank in which customers hold $100 million in checking accounts. This bank is required to hold 10 percent of this, or $10 million, in the form of vault cash or as deposits at its regional Federal Reserve bank.

A decision by the Fed to raise the required reserve ratio would require banks to hold more of their assets in the form of reserves. As banks cannot make loans out of their required reserves, such requirement would effectively cause the money supply to decline. Conversely, a reduction in the required reserve ratio would lead to an increase in the money supply. Because a change in reserve requirements can have a very powerful effect on monetary and credit conditions, the Fed rarely uses this tool for ordinary day-to-day monetary policy operations.

Further Reading

Akhtar, M. A. *Understanding Open Market Operations*. New York: Federal Reserve Bank of New York, 1997.

Bruce, Neil. *Public Finance and the American Economy*. Reading, Mass.: Addison-Wesley, 1998.

Friedman, Milton, and Anna Jacobson Schwartz. *A Monetary History of the United States, 1867–1960*. Princeton, N.J.: Princeton University Press, 1971.

—*Rich MacDonald*

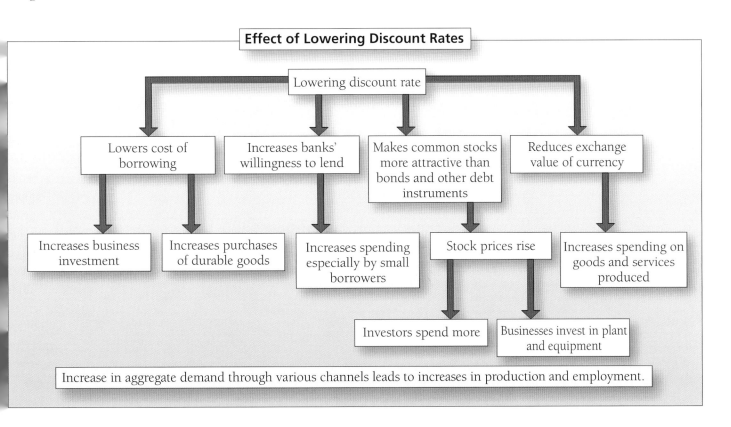

Effect of Lowering Discount Rates

Increase in aggregate demand through various channels leads to increases in production and employment.

See also:
Credit Cards and Debit Cards; Federal Reserve System; Monetary Policy.

Money

According to the lyrics of a song from a popular musical, "money makes the world go around." Why is money so important? The answer involves trade. In early civilizations and throughout history, people have found engaging in trade—exchanging something of value for something else—beneficial and have searched for ways to engage in trade efficiently and easily. Trading partners discovered that they could ease the task of trading by using certain instruments that would be commonly accepted as payment for goods and services. In other words, they developed money.

The advantages of money transactions can be gauged by a comparison with barter—exchanging goods and services directly for other goods and services. In most circumstances, bartering is inefficient, and in any barter economy, individuals find it difficult to specialize in those tasks at which they are most proficient. If the world's best mousetrap builder had a taste for tomatoes, she would have to search long and hard, in a barter economy, to identify a tomato grower wanting to purchase mousetraps. Rather than persisting in searches of that sort, the mousetrap producer would soon abandon her specialized craft to grow the tomatoes and other foods necessary for her survival. Thus, resources that are best used in producing mousetraps are inefficiently allocated to producing tomatoes.

Where money transactions are the norm, however, such inefficiencies are less likely to arise: the mousetrap builder uses the money she earns from selling mousetraps to purchase tomatoes in the marketplace. This allows her to do what she does best—to specialize. As a result, she benefits; society also benefits because money transactions of this sort encourage efficient use of scarce resources.

Money is commonly defined as an asset that is accepted as payment for goods and services or in settling debts. We know it mainly as bills, coins, and checks, but in other times and places money has taken many forms. Some ancient societies used cattle as money. Some Native Americans used wampum (beads of polished shells strung in strands). Prisoners of war used cigarettes as money during World War II. The last example shows that an asset need not be issued by a government authority to serve as money. With or without government sponsorship, monetary exchanges evolve from the desire to trade efficiently.

For an asset to serve as money, it must function as a medium of exchange. An exchange medium is directly convertible

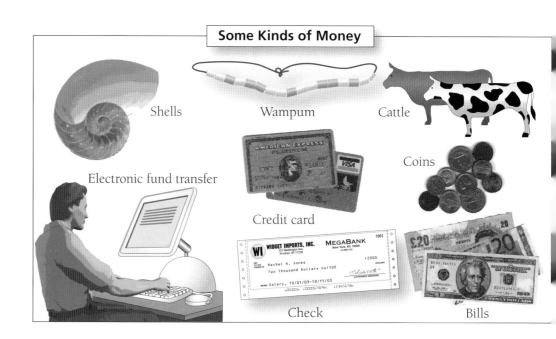

Some Kinds of Money

Shells   Wampum   Cattle

Electronic fund transfer

Credit card   Coins

Check   Bills

into goods and services. Money also serves as a unit of account (or standard of value)— money is the common unit in which market values are expressed in modern economies. Which is more valuable: a loaf of white bread or a new television set? Certainly the TV. The market value of the TV may be about 200 times that of the loaf of bread. How is this computed? By comparing the dollar price of the TV (about $200) to the dollar price of the loaf of bread (about $1). Note that this comparison is possible only because the market value of each item is expressed in a common unit, dollars.

Imagine living in a world in which a common unit did not exist. A shopper might enter a supermarket to find the price of a gallon of milk listed as 10 pencils. Another store might price milk at four cans of tuna fish. A third store might charge three loaves of bread for a gallon of milk. Which is the best deal? Impossible to determine unless exchange ratios for pencils and milk, milk and tuna, and bread and milk can be calculated. Even if such ratios could be established, using them would be difficult in a modern economy in which an enormous quantity and variety of goods and services are available.

Money must also serve as a store of value (or store of wealth). Between the time people receive money and the time they use it, people usually hold money. Money must retain its purchasing power, for the most part, during this holding period. If it did not, people would be reluctant to accept money in payment for goods and services and it would fall out of favor as an exchange medium. Money is not unique as a store of value, however. Many other assets, including stocks and bonds, real estate and jewelry, are also used to store wealth.

History provides many examples of times when rapid price increases caused money's function as a store of value to break down. In Germany after World War I, hyper-inflation ran rampant, driving prices upward at rates as high as 10 percent per hour. German government printing presses had to print money in ever-larger denominations to

A worker at the Denver Mint in 1968.

keep up with these increases (up to one-million-mark notes), and currency in smaller denominations, such as one-mark notes, became worthless. In fact, parents gave small notes to children as play money. This led to a complete economic breakdown in Germany and provided an ambitious political upstart named Adolf Hitler with an issue to exploit in his campaign for power.

Major Functions of Money

- Medium of exchange: directly convertible into goods and services
- Store of value: retains purchasing power
- Unit of account: unit in which values are stated, recorded, and settled
- Standard of deferred payment: unit in which debt contracts are stated

PayPal Chief Executive Officer Peter Thiel, left, and founder Elon Musk, right, pose with the PayPal logo at the company's headquarters in Palo Alto, California, in 2000.

In the United States, the payments system has evolved over time. Commodity money (coins minted from gold or silver) was common in the eighteenth and nineteenth centuries. Next came paper currency backed by precious commodities, then modern currency that is not convertible into precious metals, then checks, and most recently electronic funds transfers. Each means of payment has advantages and disadvantages. Commodity monies are bulky and awkward. Paper currency is easy to carry, but it provides purchasing power to anybody who holds it; therefore, thieves like to lift wallets. Checks need to be signed by the account holder before they can be used as payment, but it is quite costly (looking at the country as a whole) to process checks. Finally, payment by electronic transfer can be cost effective, but many people remain concerned about its security.

The future of money may be digital. Computers and personal digital assistants have become smaller, cheaper, and increasingly widespread, leading some analysts to predict that money as we now know it will disappear and will be replaced by "smart cards" or some other kind of digital cash. Companies like the Palo Alto–based PayPal have sprung up to provide a safe alternative to using credit cards online; the PayPal service allows anyone with an e-mail address to send and receive secure online payments. Whatever form future money takes, money itself will continue to foster human interaction through trade; for this reason, money is one of the most important inventions in human history.

Further Reading

Federal Reserve Bank of New York. *The Story of Checks and Electronic Payments.* New York: Federal Reserve Bank of New York, 1995.

———. *The Story of Money.* New York: Federal Reserve Bank of New York, 1994.

Radford, R. A. "The Economic Organization of a P.O.W. Camp." *Economica*, 12 November 1945, 189–201.

Weatherford, Jack. *The History of Money: From Sandstone to Cyberspace.* New York: Crown Publishers, 1997.

—*Rich MacDonald*

Monopoly

Monopoly is an economic condition under which a particular market is controlled by a single firm. Although many different factors can contribute to the formation of monopoly—economies of scale, patents, or government franchising, to name a few—most monopolies tend to be undesirable for a society. Usually a monopolist will produce a smaller quantity of output and charge a higher price than what would prevail under perfect competition. Although true monopolies are rare in the United States, monopolistic power, including the ability to control prices, is not.

Competition

When considering the level of competition among firms in a given market, economists distinguish between four categories of economic conditions: (1) perfect competition, (2) monopolistic competition, (3) oligopoly, and (4) monopoly. Under perfect competition, many firms exist that produce and sell homogeneous (identical) products. Because each individual seller is very small in relation to the size of the entire market, no one firm can control price. With monopolistic competition, many producers sell nonhomogeneous (differentiated) products and thus have limited control over their prices. In an oligopoly, the market is controlled by several large firms competing in the production and sale of identical products. A monopoly is an extreme form of market concentration,

where no competition exists because one producer controls the market.

Real-life examples of the extreme market conditions—perfect competition and monopoly—are rather rare; most markets can be characterized as being moderately concentrated, that is, either monopolistically competitive or oligopolistic. The market for DVD players, for example, may be described as one of monopolistic competition: many firms produce DVD players, and the products are distinguished from one another by their features. However, the world aircraft manufacturing industry has only two firms—Airbus and Boeing—and, thus, is a duopoly (a special case of oligopoly). Nevertheless, monopolies do exist and some have played very important roles in the development of the modern industrialized economies.

Sources of Monopoly Power

Although a number of factors make the emergence of monopoly more likely, one feature is common to all monopolies: barriers to entry are significant, that is, some market conditions prevent other firms from entering the industry and successfully competing with the monopolist. Any cost that must be incurred by a potential entrant into the market, but that the incumbent (a firm already in the market) does not incur, constitutes an entry barrier. Economists commonly identify two major categories of entry barriers: legal and natural.

A legal barrier to entry may be an exclusive right to produce a specific product and market it in a specific location. Such exclusive rights prevent entry by making entry

See also:
Competition; Regulation of Business and Industry; Sherman Antitrust Act.

Types of Competition

Kind of competition	Number of producers	Product differentiation	Examples	Control over price
Perfect competition	Many	Products identical	Agricultural products	None
Monopolistic competition	Many	Differentiated	DVD players	Limited
Oligopoly	Several	Identical	Aircraft	Some
Monopoly	One	One product; no substitutes available	Prozac; Postal Service	Significant

Key U.S. Antitrust Legislation

1890 Sherman Antitrust Act
- Makes illegal every contract, conspiracy or restraint of interstate trade and foreign commerce.
- Makes illegal the attempt by any person to monopolize, attempt to monopolize, or conspire to monopolize any part of interstate trade or foreign commerce.

1914 Clayton Antitrust Act
- Declares price discrimination illegal if it restricts competition.
- Outlaws restraints of trade like tying and exclusive dealing arrangements.

1914 Federal Trade Commission Act
Empowers commission to:
- Prevent unfair methods of competition and unfair or deceptive practices in commerce.
- Seek monetary redress or other relief for conduct injurious to commerce.
- Prescribe trade regulations addressing unfair and monopolistic practices and establish requirements designed to prevent such acts and practices.

1936 Robinson–Patman Act
- Expands kinds of price-fixing deemed illegal under the Clayton Act.

1950 Cellar–Kefauver Antimerger Act
- Prevents firms from merging if the effect would substantially decrease competition in an industry or tend to create a monopoly.

1976 Hart–Scott–Rodino Notification Act
- Requires firms to get FTC approval before an acquisition of any company worth more than $15 million.

illegal. A patent is one example of this kind of entry barrier: for instance, for a number of years the pharmaceutical company Eli Lilly had a patent for the production of the antidepressant drug Prozac. Another example is a government franchise, by which the government authorizes one firm to be the designated provider of a good or service in a specific region. The U.S. Postal Service is the result of such a monopoly-granting franchise. Also, a professional license—such as one required to be a dentist or to practice law—can be considered a barrier to entry. However, while such licenses restrict entry into certain occupations, they do not typically create a monopoly.

Natural entry barriers usually take one of two forms. The first is the control by the firm of a major resource necessary for the production of the good. Although such situations rarely arise in practice, two commonly cited examples are the Aluminum Company of America (Alcoa), which controlled the vast majority of bauxite (required to produce aluminum) in the pre–World War II United States, and DeBeers, which historically had access to most of the world's diamond mines located in South Africa.

The second kind of natural barrier to entry is most important in utilities, for example, electricity generation and distribution and water and gas utilities, but it is also often observed in other industries. The natural condition of some industries, known in economics as economies of scale, makes possible the achievement of a lower average cost of production by a single producer rather than by several firms sharing the industry. This phenomenon frequently occurs in industries where an entrant must make a very large initial investment to begin producing, but each additional unit beyond the first is relatively cheap to make. For example, an electric power utility must invest in generating and transmitting equipment before producing the first kilowatt, but once those are in place, producing additional units of electricity is not very costly. Similarly, one could argue that significant economies of scale occur in the software industry, where a firm must make large investments in research and development of new software, but once it is written, copying it onto more disks (producing additional units) is very cheap.

A firm that has the sole control of a market because of natural barriers to entry is sometimes called a natural monopoly. Any public utility, for instance, the Philadelphia Electric Company (PECO), is a good example. Natural monopolies are very important for policy makers because, unlike other kinds of monopolies, they may be desirable. Society may benefit by having certain industries monopolized rather than insisting on competition in every sphere.

Historical Background

Monopolies existed in ancient times, often because of extreme scarcity of some necessary input. During the Middle Ages, guilds, which were associations of merchants or craftsmen, controlled entry into their market, the output they produced, and the prices they charged. As European nation-states began to evolve into vast empires, the royal courts often granted monopoly rights to their favorite companies for the production and supply of such essential products as tobacco and salt. Foreign exploration and trade were also usually handled by state-sponsored monopolies.

However, the ideas of free market and competition, introduced by the British philosopher Adam Smith, were becoming increasingly popular in the late eighteenth and early nineteenth centuries. The new tendency in most industries was toward more producers, more competition, smaller firms, and less market control.

Large, dominating firms returned as key players in several industries in the late nineteenth century as entrepreneurs sought to build capitalist empires by driving competition out of business, using tactics considered predatory. The most famous monopoly of this period was Standard Oil, led by American businessman John D. Rockefeller. Rockefeller was notorious for his predatory strategies, including merging his company with a competitor and then using the officials from this new firm to spy on the remaining competitors. Other monopolies were created as a result of mergers among several smaller firms, yet others were so-called

In this 1871 cartoon, a man with a monopoly on coal takes on the form of the devil as he advertises his goods at outrageous prices.

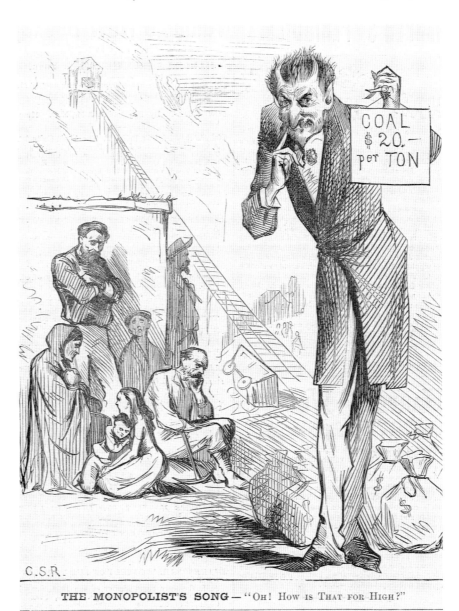

THE MONOPOLIST'S SONG — "Oh! How is That for High?"

Chronology of a Monopoly: Standard Oil

1870
John D. Rockefeller founds the Standard Oil Company in Cleveland, Ohio. The company has more than 250 competitors and accounts for less than 4 percent of the refined oil business.

1870s
Using then-legal tactics like railroad rebates and predatory pricing, as well as spying and bribery, Rockefeller persuades his competitors to sell out or join him.

1879
Rockefeller controls 90 percent of the U.S. oil refining capacity as well as large petroleum reserves and extensive oil pipelines.

1882
Rockefeller turns Standard Oil and 40 other companies in which he has interest into the Standard Oil Trust, the first trust in the United States. The trust has a virtual monopoly on U.S. oil.

1890
Congress passes the Sherman Antitrust Act in reaction to the growth of monopolies.

1892
Ohio courts order the Standard Oil Trust dissolved and 20 constituent companies are organized.

1899
Because New Jersey permits the existence of holding companies, the constituent companies are gathered into the Standard Oil Company (New Jersey).

1911
In *Standard Oil Co. v. United States*, the U.S. Supreme Court declares Standard Oil in violation of the Sherman Antitrust Act and orders the trust dissolved into 34 companies.

trusts, or groups of firms banding together to control their market.

In the twentieth century, as the U.S. government became ever more intolerant of monopolies and the monopolization of industries, examples of market domination became few. The Microsoft case, however, brought by the Department of Justice in 1998, was hotly debated in the courts as well as in the press and in academic literature. Microsoft was found to have monopolized the market for computer operating systems and used that monopoly power to establish itself in other markets, for example, Internet browsing software.

Other countries have generally taken a less strict approach to controlling monopolies.

In the United Kingdom and other European countries, antimonopoly legislation is designed to protect the public interest, which means that a monopoly resulting in public benefits is allowed to exist. This is not the case in the United States, where monopolization is illegal. At the other extreme, some countries have chosen not to fight monopolies at all; Singapore, for instance, has historically had no antitrust laws.

Theory of Monopoly

Like any other business venture, a monopoly pursues maximum profit. To maximize profit, any business must adjust the quantity of output it produces and the price it charges its customers. A common misconception is that a monopoly can charge any price it wants; another common mistake is assuming that it will try to charge the highest price possible. Both ideas are erroneous because they ignore the fact that the monopoly's control of the market is limited by two conditions: the demand for the product or service and the cost of production, which depends on such factors as technology and prices of inputs (for example, wages). Therefore, the monopoly will choose a level of output (or quantity) and price such that its profits, which are the difference between revenues and costs, are maximized. Typically, the output will be considerably smaller than that produced by a perfectly competitive industry; also, the price charged by the monopoly will usually be higher than the competitive price.

Under certain circumstances, a monopoly may be able to increase its profits through a practice known as price discrimination. This tactic, which basically involves charging different prices for different units of the same product, can take one of several forms. For example, a firm may offer quantity discounts to buyers who purchase in bulk; then customers self-select into appropriate categories according to the amount of the good they choose to buy. Such menus of prices are common for electric or water utilities; customers pay a certain price for, say, the first 500 kilowatts per month, a lower price for the next 500, and a lower price yet for any energy used above 1,000 kilowatts.

Another form of price discrimination results when a company is able to separate customers according to their willingness to pay for the good or service; for example,

A hydroelectric power plant on the Feather River in California. Electric companies sometimes bolster profits through a practice known as price discrimination.

airlines are notorious for charging business travelers higher fares than they do those who fly for leisure. In the case of air travel, it is easy to keep the two groups separate by simply requiring that round-trip leisure passengers spend Saturday night at their destination. In most cases, however, maintaining that distinction may be difficult. It can also be difficult to prevent those paying the low price from reselling the product at a higher price to the high-price group.

Treatment of Monopolies

Beginning in the late nineteenth century, the U.S. government recognized the need to be able to limit monopolies' control over production and prices to prevent harm to consumers. The Sherman Antitrust Act, passed

Barriers to Entry		
Legal	*Natural*	
Exclusive right to produce a product or market it in a specific location	Control of major resource needed for production	Economies of scale
• Patent holder (Eli Lilly for Prozac)	• Alcoa (bauxite)	• PECO (electricity)
• Government franchise (U.S. Postal Service for mail)	• DeBeers (diamonds)	• Microsoft (computer operating systems)

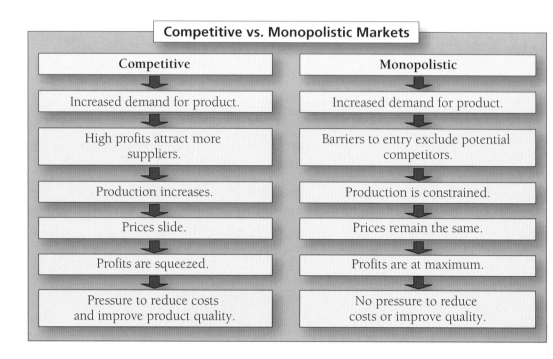

Competitive vs. Monopolistic Markets

Competitive	Monopolistic
Increased demand for product.	Increased demand for product.
High profits attract more suppliers.	Barriers to entry exclude potential competitors.
Production increases.	Production is constrained.
Prices slide.	Prices remain the same.
Profits are squeezed.	Profits are at maximum.
Pressure to reduce costs and improve product quality.	No pressure to reduce costs or improve quality.

in 1890, made any business agreement for the purpose of restricting interstate trade illegal. Other laws followed, with the Clayton Act in 1914 prohibiting mergers and interlocking directorates that lessen competition.

In 1911 the government accused Standard Oil of having a monopoly under Section II of the Sherman Act and required that the company be broken up into more than 30 smaller firms. Splitting a company into several competitors has been the standard tool for handling monopolies; for example, in the 1980s AT&T was forced to re-form itself into smaller regional Bell companies.

Some monopolies, however, do exist. In the public utility sector, for example, the government tends to regulate natural monopolies, that is, to grant the company the right to exclusive service but oversee its prices and level of service. Examples include power utilities, cable companies, and telecommunications providers. The recent trends in these industries, however, have been toward deregulation and introduction of competition.

Monopolies historically have occupied a very prominent place in many industries. Today, economists know much about the effects of monopolization; yet many questions remain. Controversial issues include the role of patents in the pharmaceutical industry, where firms are able to realize tremendous profits from sales of life-saving drugs. Some people argue that such drugs should be available to those who need them at very low prices. However, the consensus among economists seems to be that drug patents are necessary to stimulate research and development; without them, some drugs may never be developed at all. Such debates underscore the importance of monopolies in today's economies.

Further Reading

Breit, William, and Kenneth Elzinga, eds. *The Antitrust Casebook: Milestones in Economic Regulation.* 3rd ed. Fort Worth, Tex.: Dryden Press, 1996.

Bringhurst, Bruce. *Antitrust and the Oil Monopoly: The Standard Oil Cases, 1890–1911.* Westport, Conn.: Greenwood Press, 1979.

Deutsch, Larry L. "Pharmaceuticals: The Critical Role of Innovation." In *Industry Studies,* edited by Larry Deutsch. 2nd ed. Armonk, N.Y.: M. E. Sharpe, 1998.

Kwoka, John E., Jr., and Lawrence White, eds. *The Antitrust Revolution: Economics, Competition, and Policy.* 3rd ed. New York: Oxford University Press, 1999.

Mueller, Milton. *Universal Service: Competition, Interconnection, and Monopoly in the Making of the American Telephone System.* Cambridge, Mass.: MIT Press, 1997.

Schiller, Bradley R. *Essentials of Economics.* 4th ed. Boston: McGraw-Hill/Irwin, 2002.

— *Mikhail Kouliavtsev*

Morgan, J. P.

1837–1913
Financier

Progress of the scale seen during the Industrial Revolution created a new challenge in the business world: as firms grew larger and attempted more ambitious projects, they needed enormous amounts of money. James Pierpont Morgan was the man most responsible for revolutionizing banking to meet the demands of industrial-scale companies. He used his skill and influence as a banker to reduce the risk of doing business and created many of the world's largest companies in the process. His legacy includes U.S. Steel, General Electric, and the creation of the Federal Reserve System.

J. P. Morgan was born in Connecticut in 1837. He was the son of Junius Spencer Morgan, a prominent banker who became wealthy by helping rich Englishmen invest in the United States. Junius trained his son to enter his business from an early age, arranging for the best education available to prepare a young man for a future in finance. The younger Morgan took full advantage of his training and family connections by

See also:
Carnegie, Andrew; Federal Reserve System.

A portrait of J. P. Morgan from the 1890s.

starting Dabney, Morgan and Company in 1864 and rising to dominate American investment banking by 1873. He did this by outmaneuvering the leading banker of the day, Jay Cooke.

Both Cooke and Morgan had agreed to raise money for the U.S. government by selling a set amount of bonds in a certain amount of time. A banker selling these securities takes the risk that the value of the bonds might decline before they can be sold, leaving the banker with a loss. Taking advantage of his father's connections, Morgan was able to sell many of these bonds to English investors with relative ease. Cooke lacked foreign connections and was less successful. Some historians also assert that Morgan engineered a collapse in the market to reduce the value of the bonds and destroy his rival, although concrete evidence is lacking. Regardless, the result was Cooke's bankruptcy in the 1873 market panic, with Morgan emerging as the leading banker in America.

Meanwhile, the need for large-scale investment banking grew as the Industrial Revolution accelerated in the United States. Morgan became heavily involved with the financing of railroads, which needed enormous amounts of money to purchase land and lay track. His approach to railroad financing was based on his view that competition was counterproductive, driving down prices and causing redundant construction as companies vied to serve the same markets.

This competition reduced profits and made raising money more expensive for railroads.

Morgan's solution was to encourage the creation of communities of interest—agreements between railroad companies that reduced competition, decreased investment in new lines, and set prices. His actions helped stabilize the railroad industry and increase profits for both the railroads and the banks that lent them money—thus increasing profits for Morgan.

While good for business, Morgan's approach was criticized for being anticompetitive. Consumers had to pay higher prices, eventually spurring the government into action. By the early 1900s the government acted to make business cooperation illegal and broke up the railroad trusts to reduce prices.

Morgan conducted similar activities in other industries. The most famous example was the steel industry, which was dominated by Carnegie Steel but suffered from competition, high costs, and other inefficiencies. Morgan used his influence to buy a number of Carnegie's competitors and to create "order" in the business. He bought out Andrew Carnegie for the then unheard of sum of $480 million, leading to the creation of the largest corporation in the world at that time, U.S. Steel, worth more than $1 billion.

Morgan's money-raising ability and his knack for convincing business leaders to accept his leadership resulted in perhaps his greatest legacy as a guarantor of stability in

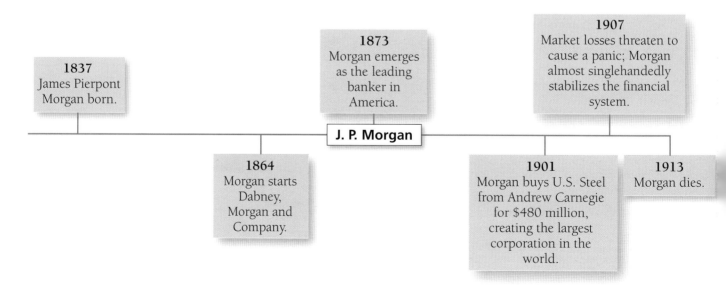

1837
James Pierpont Morgan born.

1873
Morgan emerges as the leading banker in America.

1907
Market losses threaten to cause a panic; Morgan almost singlehandedly stabilizes the financial system.

J. P. Morgan

1864
Morgan starts Dabney, Morgan and Company.

1901
Morgan buys U.S. Steel from Andrew Carnegie for $480 million, creating the largest corporation in the world.

1913
Morgan dies.

the U.S. economy. Market panics and near-collapses were common during the late nineteenth and early twentieth centuries. At this time, banks were not guaranteed against failing by the government and they often accepted stocks as collateral against loans. Therefore, if a company's stock price dropped, banks could fail as their assets became worthless and depositors rushed to withdraw their money. Urgent withdrawals could lead to runs on other banks and damage to the entire economy.

Such disorder was a direct threat to both Morgan's vision of organized capitalism and his personal fortune in banking. As a result, he used his stature and influence to calm markets during panics, most famously in 1907, when market losses resulted in large withdrawals from many banks and severe losses in the stock market. Morgan demonstrated his commanding stature by personally orchestrating the rescue of the financial system. Among other actions, he intimidated New York bankers into raising $25 million to stabilize the market. Although President Theodore Roosevelt had frequently been a critic of Morgan, he sent his treasury secretary to New York with instructions to follow Morgan's orders, resulting in the establishment of an additional $25 million line of credit to bolster the banking system.

These acts restored confidence in the banking system and the panic subsided. Morgan's preservation of the economy inspired the eventual creation of the Federal Reserve System—the nation's central bank. It uses the authority of the federal government to fulfill a role that Morgan had engineered—that of guarantor of a sound business environment.

J. P. Morgan died on March 31, 1913. His last will and testament was marked by a strong faith in Christianity, and in his will he urged his heirs to maintain the same. He left his heirs $80 million, a fraction of the wealth amassed by other tycoons of the era.

This 1902 cartoon shows people of various professions and nationalities following the piper, J. P. Morgan.

Further Reading

Chernow, Ron. *The House of Morgan: An American Banking Dynasty and the Rise of Modern Finance.* New York: Simon & Schuster, 1991.
Strouse, Jean. *Morgan: American Financier.* New York: Random House, 1999.

—*David Long*

See also:
Arts and Entertainment Industry; Cultural Difference; Globalization; Sony Corporation.

Morita, Akio

1921–1999
Cofounder, Sony Corporation

Akio Morita was the force behind the creation of communications giant Sony. Although he was not alone in founding or running the company, Morita's vision of a global company drove Sony forward.

Morita was born on January 26, 1921. He had been groomed since the third grade to become the successor to his family's 400-year-old sake brewing business in the city of Tokoname, near Nagoya. He began sitting in on company meetings with his father when he was still a boy. After graduating from the physics department at Osaka Imperial University in 1944, Morita joined the navy as a lieutenant. He was put to work conducting electronics research for the Japanese navy's Wartime Research Committee.

Eventually Morita was moved to a naval group working on thermal guidance weapons and night-vision gunsights. One of the civilian members of this group was an electronics engineer named Masaru Ibuka, who would later cofound Sony Corporation with Morita.

Morita was a nationalist, but he was also a pragmatist, and he was not afraid of a future without Japanese nationalism. He arranged to be away from his navy unit on the day of Japan's surrender to the United States in 1945, assuming that the officers would all be asked to commit ritual suicide. (He guessed correctly; many of the officers from his unit did, indeed, kill themselves.)

The Founding of Sony

When the war ended, Morita moved to Tokyo. He read an article about a research laboratory, Tokyo Telecommunications Research Institute, founded by Ibuka. Morita visited Ibuka in Tokyo and the pair decided to establish a new company together—Tokyo Tsushin Kogyo K.K. (Tokyo Telecommunications Engineering Corporation; renamed Sony in 1958), using capital from Morita's wealthy family.

The huge success of Sony's transistor radio (first marketed in 1957) made Sony a powerful company. While other Japanese companies were still thinking in national terms, Morita was interested in creating a worldwide brand. The name Sony, from the Latin word *sonus* (sound), was specifically chosen because it is pronounceable in any language.

From the outset, Morita's marketing concept for Sony was brand-name identification and brand responsibility: he wanted the name Sony to instantly communicate high quality. This is now a common marketing concept, but in 1950s Japan most companies were either copying existing American technology or producing under somebody else's brand name. Pentax, for example, was making products for Honeywell, Ricoh for Savin, and Sanyo for Sears.

In 1960 Morita and Ibuka established Sony Corporation of America. Morita spent one year living in the United States with his wife

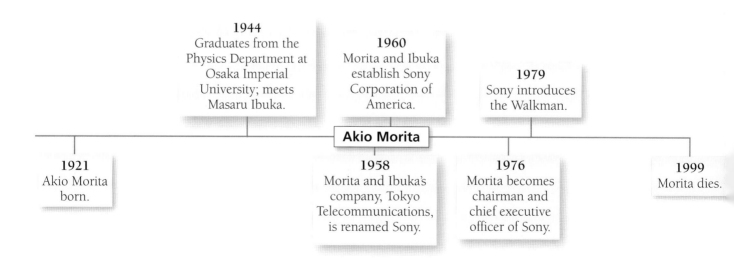

1944
Graduates from the Physics Department at Osaka Imperial University; meets Masaru Ibuka.

1960
Morita and Ibuka establish Sony Corporation of America.

1979
Sony introduces the Walkman.

Akio Morita

1921
Akio Morita born.

1958
Morita and Ibuka's company, Tokyo Telecommunications, is renamed Sony.

1976
Morita becomes chairman and chief executive officer of Sony.

1999
Morita dies.

and children immersing himself in American culture to understand what products America wanted. This understanding of American culture allowed Morita to develop an intuition about electronic products that would appeal to both Americans and Japanese. For example, the Walkman personal stereo was released in 1979, inspired by Morita's observations of how much time Americans spent lugging large stereos around to beaches and parties.

A Global Outlook

Morita encouraged a global outlook throughout his career. In the 1960s he began speaking about issues like free trade and reducing tariffs and other barriers, ideas Japanese businessmen had been reluctant to discuss for decades.

In 1976 Morita became chairman and CEO of Sony Corporation. He led the company through a period when Japanese imports dominated the U.S. consumer market. He represented, very vocally, the business community of Japan, a country that had during the 1970s become the second leading economy in the world.

Morita was famous in the United States for his cosmopolitan outlook; in Japan he remained a patriot. That became evident in 1989, when he coauthored the book, *A Japan That Can Say No*, in which he suggested that other countries should stop complaining about the high quality of Japanese imports and get to work improving their own corporations. The book caused outrage in the United States, although Morita had intended it for a Japanese audience. He had hoped to convince the consensus-oriented Japanese to see that in other countries disagreement and debate were not insulting and that Japanese could argue with their foreign business partners without destroying their friendship.

Although he was the marketing force behind products like the videocassette recorder (VCR), the transistorized TV, the Walkman, and metal audiotape, Morita's intuition was not perfect. Although Sony invented the VCR, marketing errors led to the VHS replacing Sony's Betamax as the VCR standard. Morita championed global culture; nevertheless, many decisions at Sony were made out of a desire to please Morita—an old-fashioned Japanese style

Sony chairman Akio Morita in 1989.

of management. For example, the 1989 decision to buy a vastly overpriced Columbia Pictures was made after Morita expressed regret at a company dinner that Sony did not yet own a movie studio. Sony eventually lost more than $3 billion on Columbia.

Morita was driven in every aspect of his life. He followed art and music and was a sports fanatic. In his 60s he took up wind surfing and scuba diving and started skiing to ensure good exercise through the winter. He loved to water-ski and even invented a water-resistant microphone on a handle that was connected by a wire on the ski rope to a speaker on the boat so he could relay instructions to his wife. At 72, he was still playing tennis at 7 A.M. every Tuesday. On November 30, 1993, Morita suffered a stroke while playing tennis; he retired as head of Sony in 1994. His health remained poor, and he succumbed to pneumonia on October 3, 1999.

Further Reading

Hurst, G. Cameron. *Saying "No" to America: The Morita-Ishihara Critique of the U.S.* Indianapolis, Ind.: Universities Field Staff International, 1990.

Morita, Akio, with Edwin M. Reingold and Mitsuko Shimomura. *Made in Japan: Akio Morita and Sony.* New York: Signet, 1988.

Nathan, John. *Sony: The Private Life.* Boston: Houghton Mifflin, 1999.

—Lisa Magloff

See also:
Edison, Thomas Alva;
Telecommunications Industry.

Morse, Samuel

1791–1872
Inventor of the telegraph

Samuel Morse was a nineteenth-century portrait painter, politician, art professor, school administrator, promoter, divinity student, and amateur architect. His invention of the electric telegraph overshadowed all his other achievements, for it began a communications revolution and showed that electricity could be harnessed to do an important job.

Samuel Finley Breese Morse was born April 27, 1791, to Elizabeth Breese Morse and Pastor Jedidiah Morse, author of the first geography book printed in the United States. Samuel Morse grew up in Charlestown, Massachusetts, although he spent much of his youth attending private schools in other locales. He was fascinated with the new discovery of electricity while in school; he also found he had a passion and talent for art. After graduation from Yale College in 1810, he sailed for England in 1811 to study art in London. He returned home in 1815 because his parents declined to fund his stay any longer.

When several exhibitions of his work were unsuccessful, Morse began concentrating on one of the few artistic fields in which self-sufficiency was possible: portraiture. He traveled around the eastern United States painting portraits of prominent citizens of various towns, earning a reasonable income but never getting ahead. During this time he also seriously considered studying for a career in the Christian church, competed with others to furnish the design for a building at Andover Seminary, and did the drawings for a patent on an improved water pump his brother Sidney had designed for fire departments. He also began work on a marble-carving device intended to allow the carver to duplicate a statue. These endeavors reflected both his need to make an income and his restless intellect.

Morse moved to New York but received few portrait commissions at first. In 1825 he was commissioned by the city to do a portrait of Marquis de Lafayette, a French hero of the American Revolution. The Lafayette commission led to other portrait orders and eventually to Morse's cofounding of the National Academy of Design in 1826, where he meant to teach aspiring artists as well as raise public awareness of the importance of art.

In 1829 Morse began a tour of Europe, including time spent enjoying the many paintings of Italy, as well as those in the Louvre in Paris, France. This visit only confirmed Morse's feelings that Americans did not care enough about the arts, and he resolved to do even more to educate Americans about art when he returned home.

Samuel Morse poses with his telegraph around 1850; photograph by Mathew Brady.

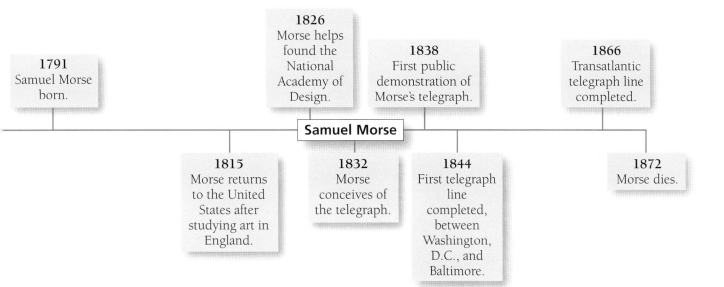

1791
Samuel Morse born.

1826
Morse helps found the National Academy of Design.

1838
First public demonstration of Morse's telegraph.

1866
Transatlantic telegraph line completed.

Samuel Morse

1815
Morse returns to the United States after studying art in England.

1832
Morse conceives of the telegraph.

1844
First telegraph line completed, between Washington, D.C., and Baltimore.

1872
Morse dies.

The return voyage to the United States in 1832, however, would transform Morse from promoter of the arts to inventor. In a conversation en route discussing recent discoveries about electricity, Morse learned that electricity passed through a wire instantaneously, no matter what the length. He immediately said that if that were true, then intelligence could be transmitted across a distance by electricity. Others had thought the same thing, but as he was an amateur, Morse thought the idea was his alone and proceeded excitedly on that basis. While still on the ship he began to sketch designs for an apparatus for sending messages across great distances. The design he settled on, without access to any scientific instruments, involved a weak permanent magnet and a strong electromagnet. This would ultimately be the essence of the electric telegraph.

Unfortunately, when he got to the United States, the demands of running the Academy, making a living painting, attending to his responsibilities as a professor of painting at the University of the City of New York, writing political articles, and running for mayor of New York City left him little time to perfect his design, especially given his lack of scientific knowledge or mechanical aptitude. Crucial to the eventual development of the telegraph were Leonard Gale, a professor of chemistry at the university, and Alfred Vail, who contributed financial resources, mechanical skills, and a family-owned iron works that could fashion model telegraphs.

Other forms of electric telegraphs had been put in use but had proved to be impractical. One of them needed 26 different electric lines, one for each letter of the alphabet; the simplest still made use of five lines. Morse and the others came up with a design needing just one line between transmitter and receiver. Working with his original two-magnet design from the transatlantic voyage, the Morse electric telegraph consisted of a metal bar with a permanent magnet at one end and an electromagnet at the other end. Pulses of current from the transmitter caused the electromagnet in the receiver to move, which in turn moved a marker, which then produced a code on a strip of paper.

Morse began with a number code for each word, but this required a codebook at each end of the line. The switch to a code for each letter, consisting of some combination of long and short electric impulses, along with a change from embossing paper to sending so-called dots and dashes that could be heard and decoded by ear, produced a system that could easily transmit 40 to 50 words a minute.

In 1838 Morse gave a public demonstration of his invention but did not receive funds from Congress until 1843, when he

The telegraph used by Samuel Morse in 1844; photograph taken in 1925.

built a line between Washington, D.C., and Baltimore. The line was officially opened on May 24, 1844, with the message "What hath God wrought?"

By 1850 the United States had 12,000 miles of telegraph lines; in 1858 a transatlantic cable was laid and a message completed between the United States and Great Britain. During the Civil War the telegraph was used to communicate between troops and commanders, and President Abraham Lincoln got news from the battlefields and sent messages directly to his generals using Morse code. In 1866 a submarine telegraph line was laid across the floor of the Atlantic Ocean. Morse himself turned to philanthropic pursuits, dividing his time between New York City and a country estate near Poughkeepsie, New York. He died in 1872.

Morse's invention helped initiate the age of mass communication. Just as important, it proved there was a practical use for what had been until then a laboratory curiosity: electricity. Inspired by Morse's invention, many other inventors searched for ways to harness this powerful force, including Alexander Graham Bell with his telephone and Thomas Edison with his long list of inventions, including the electric lightbulb, electric phonograph, and motion pictures.

Further Reading

Mabee, Carleton. *The American Leonardo: A Life of Samuel F. B. Morse.* New York: Octagon Books, 1969.
Staiti, Paul J. *Samuel F. B. Morse.* Cambridge: Cambridge University Press, 1989.

—*Gary Baughr*

Mortgage

A mortgage is an interest-accruing loan granted to an individual or business for a pre-determined period of time for the purpose of buying a home, building, land, or other real estate. This loan is typically given by banks and mortgage companies and is approved only after the lender has determined that the borrower is able and willing to repay the loan. The real estate itself is used as collateral for the loan, and if, at any point, the borrower fails to make payment, the lender can force the sale of the property and return of its money. Such action is called foreclosure.

Before the 1950s personal debt was very rare. Most people paid for everything in cash, including homes. While businesses and farmers did borrow frequently, the average person did not. After World War II, when soldiers returned from war, housing was in short supply and prices for homes rose drastically. Very few people had the money to buy a home, and banks (subsidized through various government-assistance programs) began to lend money for the purpose of buying a home. As prices for homes remained high, mortgages became more common. Today, almost every home is purchased using a mortgage.

Obtaining a Mortgage

When individuals or businesses approach a financial institution for a mortgage, they most often find a specific property they would like to buy and are ready to do so. In some cases, the buyer will approach a lender before finding a property to buy to get a preapproval for a mortgage. Most lenders, before agreeing to a loan, require that the borrower have a certain amount of savings of his or her own, which will be used as the down payment for the purchase—the ideal amount for the down payment is usually 20 percent of the purchase price, but mortgages can be obtained with as little as 5 percent down payment and, in some special circumstances, even less. For example, if the buyer posts a portion of a personal portfolio (stocks and bonds) as collateral, the lender may allow the buyer to borrow the entire purchase price of the house.

A wide variety of mortgage providers are available to borrowers, but most mortgage lending is done by two kinds of lenders. Mortgage originators are companies that open a mortgage with a borrower and then, as soon as the mortgage is completed, sell it to a large bank that manages portfolios of mortgages. Mortgage originators earn a small percentage (typically around 0.15 to 0.25 percent) of the mortgage as a fee for generating the business for the large bank. Large banks also open mortgages themselves. The benefit to the large bank is that it does not have to pay a mortgage originator a fee for initiating the mortgage.

Borrowers are asked to provide documentation about employment, income, credit history, and other loans or debts. If all criteria are met, an appraisal of the real estate will be performed to confirm the value of the property, thus assuring the lender about recouping the loan in case of foreclosure.

Once the lender determines the investment is a sound one, a mortgage is granted. As a contractual agreement, a mortgage is very specific, listing in detail the amount of the loan, the interest rate charged, the repayment terms, and the length of the loan. (Mortgages are usually given for 15, 20, or 30 years.) The borrower and lender, upon agreeing to all terms of the mortgage, will have a meeting called a closing, where all documents will be signed by both parties and the actual exchange of funds takes place.

Making Mortgage Payments

The amount of each monthly payment is outlined in the mortgage agreement, including where to send the payment and when payment is due. Most agreements

See also:
Credit; Interest; Real
Estate Industry.

	Mortgage Schedule			
Month	Principal	Interest	Payment	Decrease in principal
1	$200,000.00	$1,166.67	$1,550	$383.33
2	$199,616.67	$1,164.43	$1,550	$385.57
198	$52,000.00	$303.33	$1,550	$1,246.67

include a late fee for payments that are made after a certain date of the month (for example, after the tenth day of the month). This payment consists of two figures: the principal and the interest. The principal is the amount of the actual loan. For example, a family buying a home for $250,000, with a 20 percent down payment, takes out a mortgage for $200,000 at 7 percent interest for 20 years. The principal is the amount borrowed, in this case $200,000.

Interest is the fee the lender charges for the use of its money. In this example, the interest rate is 7 percent. The interest is calculated based on the principal amount outstanding at the beginning of the month. In the early stages of the mortgage, the interest portion of the monthly payments is relatively high compared with the interest portion of the mortgage in the later months. For example, assume each monthly payment is $1,550. A portion of this repayment to the lender is interest and a portion is principal. The portion attributed to interest is calculated as follows:

Principal (start of the month) × Interest Rate
× Portion of the year

In this case, the interest portion of the payment in the first month is $1,166.67 ($200,000 × .07 × [1/12 of one year]). Therefore, $383.33 ($1,550 − $1,166.67) of the payment is the principal portion. The next month, the calculation is similar. First, one must calculate the new principal outstanding: $199,616.67 ($200,000 − $383.33), then apply the same formula used in the prior month.

The interest portion of the payment in the second month is $1,164.43 ($199,616.67 × .07 × [1/12 of one year]). Therefore, $385.57 ($1,550 − $1,164.43) of the payment is the principal portion. Notice that the interest portion in the second month is slightly smaller than the first month because the mortgage balance, or principal, has decreased slightly.

Finally, assume that it is the 198th month and the principal amount is now $52,000. The next month's interest portion of the $1,550 payment is $303.33 ($52,000 × .07 × [1/12 of one year]), and the principal portion is $1,246.67 ($1,550 − $303.33). Note that the interest portion is dramatically smaller at this time because the mortgage amount has decreased significantly. Banks typically provide the borrower with tables that contain the details of each payment for the entire mortgage.

Selecting a Mortgage Type

Although several different kinds of mortgages are available, the most common are fixed-rate and adjustable-rate mortgages. Each bank decides the rate of interest it will charge for the use of its money. With a fixed-rate mortgage, the interest rate is set and remains constant throughout the life of the loan. It will not and cannot be changed, regardless of what changes the market may see or what rates were in the past or will be in the future. This kind of mortgage appeals to many people, because they feel safe knowing how much their mortgage payments will be each month for the next 15, 20, or 30 years. People also are comforted knowing that if interest rates

Some Kinds of Mortgages	
Fixed rate	Interest rate never changes; monthly payment remains the same over life of the loan.
	Mortgages are usually for 15 or 30 years.
Adjustable-rate mortgage (ARM)	Interest rate changes to reflect changes in the credit market.
	"Cap" sets upper limit above which the interest rate cannot go.
	Amount interest rate can rise annually is limited.
Balloon loan	Money is borrowed for a time (e.g., 3, 5 or 7 years) and the loan amortized as if it were a 30-year loan.
	After the end of the period, the borrower owes the bank the remaining principal.
Hybrid loan	Interest is fixed for a specific period and then the loan converts to an ARM.
COFI (cost of funds index) loan	Interest rate is tied to the rate that banks pay their depositors. Interest rate changes monthly.

The traditional method of applying for a mortgage is in person; more and more, people are applying for mortgages via the Internet.

ncrease, which is likely, they will keep their lower rate. If rates decrease, however, home owners can refinance, or take out a new mortgage at the new lower rate, and then use that money to pay off the old higher-rate mortgage. Although such refinancing will result in lower monthly payments for the home owner, banks ordinarily charge a transaction fee to change the terms of a loan.

An adjustable-rate mortgage (ARM) has an interest rate that changes. As the market changes, interest rates go up and down. With an adjustable-rate mortgage, the interest rate can be changed periodically, usually at the end of six months or one year. If the market warrants higher interest rates, the rate on such a mortgage will increase, thereby causing monthly payments to increase. If rates drop, monthly payments would decrease. Typically, ARMs contain caps, a very valuable feature to the borrower, whereby the rate on the mortgage cannot rise above a certain amount, no matter the market rates.

The Internet and Mortgages

The Internet has streamlined the mortgage selection and approval process. In the past, a prospective buyer would have to call several companies to gather interest rate and fee information. Now, a prospective home buyer can simply enter some general information into a Web site, and within seconds, several quotes are returned on a single page with bank names and contact numbers.

Furthermore, once a mortgage company is chosen, the buyer can enter personal information (salary, existing debt, and employer, for example) onto the mortgage company's Web site to seek a preapproval. Usually within a day, the mortgage lender responds with a preapproval letter or a rejection notice; in the past, this process took several days. Eventually, through the proliferation of the Internet, a borrower will not even need to talk to anyone throughout the entire mortgage process.

Mortgages help people achieve their goals. A young couple wants to buy a first home. A company needs a building for office space. A contractor wants a plot of land on which to build a new townhouse development. Without a mortgage, these projects would be difficult, if not impossible.

Further Reading

Irwin, Robert. *Buy Your First Home!* Chicago: Dearborn, 2000.
Tyson, Eric, and Ray Brown. *Home Buying for Dummies.* New York: Hungry Minds, 2001.
Tyson, Eric, et al. *Mortgages for Dummies.* Hoboken, N.J.: John Wiley & Sons, 1999.

—*David Korb and Andréa Korb*

See also:
Cultural Difference;
Environmentalism;
Globalization; International
Trade.

Multinational Corporation

Although some companies sell their products in a strictly local or national market, many companies have tried to increase sales by selling in foreign markets. Companies may simply export the same goods they sell at home to other countries, or they might license their brand names to foreign manufacturers who build and sell goods in their home country. True multinational corporations take matters a step further, establishing some combination of actual manufacturing, distribution, and sales, or other operations in more than one country.

By the end of the twentieth century, most large companies were multinationals—a development that has not been viewed with equanimity in all quarters. Becoming a multinational can open new markets to firms, and the increased sales and flexibility that come with having operations abroad can help them cut costs and improve efficiency. Multinational companies, also called transnational companies, are also to a certain degree outside the control of any one national government. The large numbers of multinationals complicate efforts to shape the economy of any one country.

The Evolution of Multinationals

Multinational companies have a long history in the United States. Pioneering U.S. firms like Singer Sewing Machine Company established manufacturing plants abroad as early as the 1860s. During the 1920s, more and more U.S. companies established operations in foreign countries, especially in Europe.

The severe economic recession of the 1930s and the war that followed forced U.S. companies into retreat. When World War II ended in the mid-1940s, U.S.–backed agreements were put into place that encouraged international commerce, which was seen as vital to the rebuilding of Europe. Once again, U.S. companies led the charge abroad; by the late 1960s most multinationals were based in the United States.

The 1970s and 1980s saw a substantial increase in the presence of European and Japanese multinationals, which made serious inroads into the U.S. market and posed a significant competitive threat to U.S. firms. This sparked something of a nationalist backlash in the United States, with U.S. companies emphasizing their American roots. Most contemporary multinationals describe themselves as "global"

U.S. Multinational Companies 1998
(in billions of dollars)

Industry	U.S. parents				Foreign affiliates			
	Total assets	Sales	Employment (1,000)	Total employee compensation	Total assets	Sales	Employment (1,000)	Total employee compensation
All industries	9,700	5,026	20,068	926	4,001	2,443	8,388	271
Petroleum	406	289	436	28	342	340	242	12
Manufacturing	2,929	2,300	8,696	478	962	1,087	4,653	141
Wholesale trade	228	423	738	34	244	439	601	28
Finance, insurance, and real estate	4,227	628	1,200	92	1,794	154	240	14
Services	387	266	3,044	95	194	150	1,087	41
Other industries	1,522	1,121	5,954	200	444	272	1,566	36

Note: A U.S. parent is a U.S. person or business enterprise that owns or controls 10 percent or more of the voting securities of an incorporated foreign business enterprise, or an equivalent interest in an unincorporated foreign business enterprise. A foreign affiliate is a foreign business enterprise owned or controlled by the U.S. parent company.
Source: U.S. Bureau of Economic Analysis, *Survey of Current Business,* July 2000.

companies, suggesting that their home country is the world at large.

Managing a Multinational

Building and running a multinational corporation are complicated. Language barriers must be surmounted and cultural differences must be negotiated. In some cases, countries have laws limiting foreign ownership of or foreign investment in businesses, although these can usually be circumvented by establishing independently owned subsidiaries. Having operations in many different countries exposes a company to different political or currency crises that can pose a threat to business. During times of nationalist feeling, for example, multinational corporations are sometimes singled out as symbols of foreign domination.

Even without crises, multinational corporations face certain challenges, largely because of the difficultly of controlling operations that occur half a world away. A company based in San Diego, for example, must make a greater effort to monitor a factory located in Munich, Germany, than one located down the street.

One approach is to have a very centralized chain of command—the San Diego company can send executives from San Diego to run the Munich plant, using the same techniques and strategies used in San Diego. Most successful multinationals have learned to fragment control, recruiting people in Munich to run the factory there, for example. In many cases a company tries to ensure that operations abroad fit into a worldwide business plan, but some multinationals exercise very little control over their foreign operations, demanding only that profits be kept high.

Decentralizing control is sometimes referred to as being a "global" strategy (rather than an "international" one) and is considered preferable for a number of reasons. Local management of a multinational's operations usually helps defuse potential cultural tensions—local managers know the language and customs, they know how the

Revenues: Nations vs. Multinationals		
	Revenue (in billion U.S. dollars)	Year
United States	1,722.0	1998
Germany	977.0	1998
Italy	559.0	1998
United Kingdom	487.7	1998
Japan	407.0	1998
France	222.0	1998
Netherlands	163.0	1998
General Motors	161.3	1999
DaimlerChrysler	154.6	1999
Brazil	151.0	1998
Ford Motor	144.4	1999
Wal-Mart	139.2	1999
Canada	121.3	1998
Spain	113.0	1998
Sweden	109.4	1998
Mitsui	109.4	1999
Itochu	108.7	1999
Mitsubishi	107.1	1999
Exxon	100.7	1999
General Electric	100.5	1999
South Korea	100.4	1998
Toyota Motor	99.7	1999
Royal Dutch/Shell Group	93.7	1999
Marubeni	93.6	1999
Australia	90.70	1998
Sumitomo	89.0	1999
AXA	78.7	1999

Source: 1999 Fortune Global 500 Fortune; and CIA World Factbook, 1999, http://www.globalpolicy.org/socecon/tncs/tncstat2.htm (February 21, 2003).

labor market is structured, and they have a better idea of what regulators care about.

In addition, a multinational will more easily recruit talented people abroad if they know that their nationality will not pose a barrier to promotion. In contrast, if all the high-ranking executives at the Munich plant are from San Diego, any ambitious and enterprising German at the plant will go work somewhere else where the prospects for promotion are better.

An even more decentralized business model is common among industries like apparel—for example, the Oregon-based shoemaker Nike. With apparel like athletic

The production line at a Nike factory in Chi Chu, Vietnam. In 2002 Nike was Vietnam's largest private employer.

shoes, what makes a particular brand desirable tends to be the design of the shoes, not how they are manufactured. So Nike relies on independent contractors in other countries to make its shoes. This way of doing business requires Nike to work closely with its contractors to make sure quality remains high. In recent years, however, the company has attracted substantial criticism from labor activists who charge that Nike and other multinationals do not adequately monitor their contract manufacturers to ensure that they do not abuse workers.

Multinational corporations can also choose to take an international outlook regarding the products they sell, adjusting the presentation depending on the particular market.

Local tastes vary, and a company generally will sell more products if they are tailored to fit local preferences. Such customizing is a common practice among makers of foods, as food traditions vary widely from place to place and most people feel very strongly about what they are willing to eat. India has a large Hindu population that does not eat beef, so McDonald's restaurants there offer sandwiches made with lamb. The Domino's Pizza restaurant chain has had great success in Japan by offering pizza topped with mayonnaise. Customization does not work as well with, for example, heavy industrial machinery, but for restaurant companies, it costs roughly the same to top a pizza with mayonnaise as it does to top it with tomato sauce, so whatever sells pizza is used.

Pros and Cons of Multinationals

Multinationals also tend to locate different kinds of business operations in different countries because each country may offer a different advantage. Many European pharmaceutical companies, for example, have research and development facilities in the United States to take advantage of the well-educated work force.

This practice gets far more controversial, however, when it involves manufacturing jobs that, unlike the production of pharmaceuticals, do not require highly specialized skills. No special education is required to perform tasks like putting together parts on an assembly line, thus multinational corporations tend to seek the cheapest workers. Multinationals, accordingly, locate factories in poorer countries where wages tend to be very low and environmental and labor regulations lax. The United States has lost much of its manufacturing base since the 1950s because many companies have discovered that they can save a great deal of money by locating factories in countries with lower prevailing wages.

The mobility of multinationals is a source of great concern to many labor and environmental activists, who worry that multinationals will trigger a "race to the bottom" among countries. As multinationals often seek out cheap labor, labor activists worry that countries that want to attract and keep multinationals will try to keep labor costs down by banning labor unions and allowing unsafe work conditions. Environmental activists worry that multinationals will force countries to weaken environmental regulations because such regulations add to the cost of doing business.

Multinationals have benefited from government behavior that protected business interests. Some notorious incidents occurred in Nigeria throughout the 1990s, when numerous protests against pollution caused by the oil operations of Royal Dutch Shell were viciously put down by the Nigerian government, which in 1995 executed several

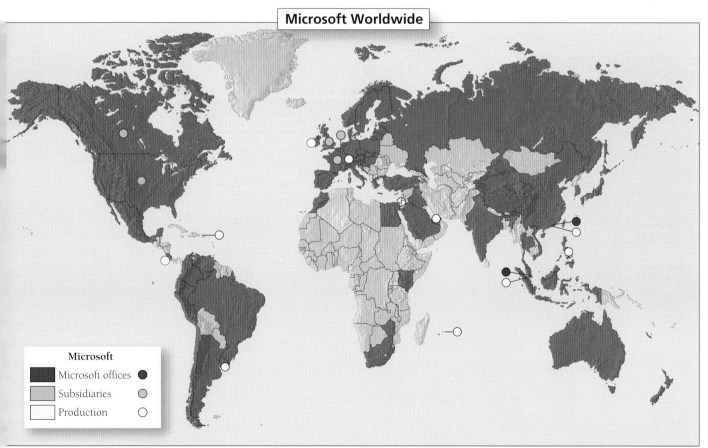

Microsoft Worldwide

Microsoft
- Microsoft offices ●
- Subsidiaries ◐
- Production ○

Source: http://www.microsoft.com/worldwide/ (February 21, 2003); and Transnational Corporations Observatory, http://www.transnationale.org/anglais/fiches/45.htm (February 21, 2003).

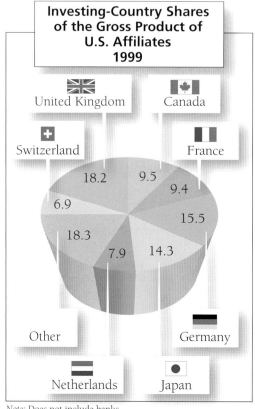

Investing-Country Shares of the Gross Product of U.S. Affiliates 1999

United Kingdom 18.2

Canada 9.5

Switzerland 6.9

France 9.4

15.5

18.3

7.9

14.3

Other

Germany

Netherlands

Japan

Note: Does not include banks.
Source: William J. Zeile, "U.S. Affiliates of Foreign Companies: Operations in 1999," *Survey of Current Business,* August 2001, http://www.bea.gov/bea/ARTICLES/2001/08august/0801FDIUS.pdf (February 24, 2003).

Ogoni activists including Ken Saro-Wiwa. Saro-Wiwa's family sued Shell in 2001, charging that the company was responsible for the executions, an allegation the company denies. One weapon activists have is publicity; indeed, the publicity surrounding Saro-Wiwa's death was enough to force Shell to pull out of Ogoni territory.

National economic policies are complicated by the fact that multinationals may build something in one country, sell it in a second country, and be based in a third country. For example, a country might want to lower unemployment, so its trade ministers might negotiate favorable trade pacts with other countries, hoping that boosting exports will lead to more hiring at home. The multinationals headquartered in the country do sell more abroad—but unemployment in the country remains the same because the multinationals' manufacturing operations are also located abroad. In addition, a multinational corporation that strongly objects to a country's economic policies can just move elsewhere—a

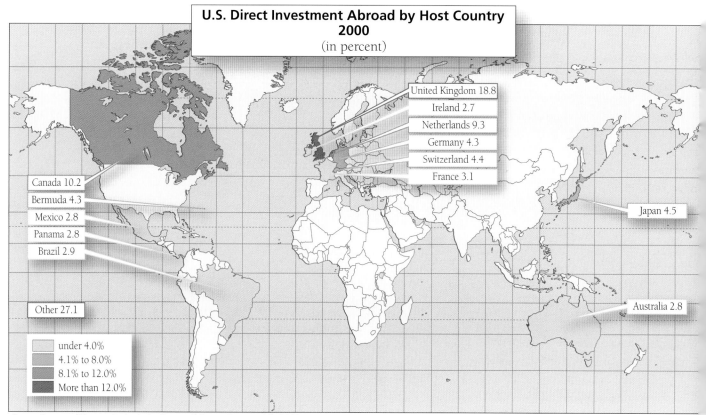

U.S. Direct Investment Abroad by Host Country 2000
(in percent)

United Kingdom 18.8

Ireland 2.7

Netherlands 9.3

Germany 4.3

Switzerland 4.4

France 3.1

Canada 10.2

Bermuda 4.3

Mexico 2.8

Panama 2.8

Brazil 2.9

Other 27.1

Japan 4.5

Australia 2.8

under 4.0%
4.1% to 8.0%
8.1% to 12.0%
More than 12.0%

Source: Bureau of Economic Analysis, *Survey of Current Business,* July 2001, http://www.bea.gov/bea/ARTICLES/2002/07july/0701dip.pdf (February 21, 2003).

significant problem for countries like Sweden with high corporate taxes.

However, the rise of multinational corporations has also created many benefits. For all the debate about conditions in factories in poorer countries, for the people who live there, factory work generally represents a major step up from subsistence farming, for example. Countries like Mexico and South Korea that once attracted the lowest-paying factory work can leverage the experience and education their workers get in industry to move up the ladder and attract skilled and better-paying manufacturing jobs.

In addition, the breaking down of national barriers has led to the spread of new and innovative ways of doing business. In the 1980s, for example, Japanese multinationals made serious inroads into U.S. markets. Although the competitive pressure was hardly welcomed, U.S. companies began to study their Japanese counterparts and discovered many clearly superior management and manufacturing practices. These practices were eventually adopted by many U.S. companies, making them stronger in the long run. For many supporters of multinationals the flow of ideas across cultural barriers is a major appeal of multinational corporations—they seem to embody the benefits of global cooperation, as opposed to nationalist hostility and competition. Especially in Europe, trade across borders has explicitly been promoted as a way to promote peace and stability. The rise of multinational corporations has hardly led to the end of war, but multinationals have, for good or ill, made the world a smaller, more interconnected place.

Further Reading

Buckley, Peter J., and Pervez N. Ghauri, eds. *The Internationalization of the Firm: A Reader.* 2nd ed. London: International Thomson Business Press, 1999.

Jonnard, Claude M. *International Business and Trade: Theory, Practice, and Policy.* Boca Raton, Fla.: St. Lucie Press, 1998.

Pitelis, Christos N., and Roger Sugden, eds. *The Nature of the Transnational Firm.* 2nd ed. London: Routledge, 2000.

Taylor, William C., and Alan M. Webber. *Going Global: Four Entrepreneurs Map the New World Marketplace.* New York: Viking, 1996.

—*Mary Sisson*

Hundreds of women of the Ijaw tribe occupied a ChevronTexaco oil export terminal at Escravos, Nigeria, for more than a week in 2002. The women demanded jobs for their relatives as well as electricity, water, and other amenities. Here, the women escort a Chevron worker who had been held hostage, as they allow him to leave.

See also:
Finance, Personal; Savings and Investment Options; Stocks and Bonds.

Mutual Funds

Mutual funds are investment vehicles managed by some investment companies. These companies pool money provided to them by individuals and then invest that money in a portfolio of stocks, bonds, or other securities. Each individual who invests money in the fund purchases shares of the investment company. The price, or net asset value (NAV), of the shares is determined by the market value of all of the investment company's assets. The NAV changes daily as the prices of the underlying stocks and bonds fluctuate in the market. As shareholders, investors own a small piece of each asset that the investment company owns.

The term *mutual fund* has become common in the past few decades because of a period of spectacular growth in mutual fund investments since 1985. In 2001 more than 8,000 mutual funds were available to investors. These funds served a variety of investment objectives by means of investment instruments that range from low-risk government bonds to high-risk technology funds. According to the Investment Company Institute, U.S. households invested $446 billion in mutual funds in 2000. As of October 2001 the Institute estimated that 52 percent of all U.S. households owned mutual funds.

Kinds of Mutual Funds

Kind	Characteristics
Aggressive growth funds	• Include riskier stocks that the manager believes will offer higher-than-average returns • Little or no dividend • May leverage assets by borrowing funds • May trade in stock options • High volatility
Growth funds	• Invest in larger stocks and industries with strong positions in their market, stable earnings, and good growth prospects • Generally surpass the S&P 500 during bull markets and do worse during bear markets • Volatile
Growth-income funds	• Invest in blue-chip stocks • Work to maximize dividend income while generating capital gains • More diversified than other kinds of funds
Income funds	• Invest in securities that pay both dividends and interest • Focus on high current income
Asset allocation funds	• Invest beyond the stock market, focusing on stocks, bonds, gold, real estate, and money market funds • Decrease reliance on one aspect of the economy
Bond funds	• Invest in corporate and government bonds • Seek high current income
Sector funds	• Invest in one sector, or industry, in the economy, e.g., biotech, communications • May underperform more diversified funds if the sector hits hard times
International funds	• Invest in foreign securities • Funds exist for individual countries or sections of the world
Precious metal funds	• Invest in gold, silver, and platinum • Generally move in opposite direction from stock market

Some investment companies that manage mutual funds are also known as open-end companies because these mutual funds continually sell shares to, and buy (redeem) shares from, the investing public at NAV. Mutual funds do not have a fixed number of shares outstanding, and they continually issue new shares. The NAV of mutual funds is computed once a day, after the close of the U.S. stock exchanges. Therefore, when an investor submits a buy or sell order to a mutual fund during the trading day, the order is filled at the NAV computed at the end of the trading day. In contrast, closed-end mutual fund companies have a fixed number of shares outstanding, and these shares trade on exchanges—much in the way individual shares of stock trade on exchanges. The shares of closed-end funds trade continually throughout the trading day at prices determined by the supply and demand for the shares. Therefore, closed-end fund shares may trade for prices above or below their NAV.

Mutual funds can be categorized by a given fund's management. Passively managed funds, also known as index funds, use an index like the S&P 500. The S&P 500 index tracks the prices of 500 stocks that trade in the U.S. stock market. An index fund based on the S&P 500 owns the 500 stocks in the index, and the composition of the index fund changes only when the companies in the S&P 500 index change. Managers of actively managed funds buy and sell securities in an attempt to achieve high returns and outperform benchmark indexes like the S&P 500.

Percent of Families Owning Mutual Funds 1992 to 1998	
1992, total	10.4
1995, total	12.3
1998, total	16.5
Age	
Under 35 years old	12.2
35–44 years old	16.0
45–54 years old	23.0
55–64 years old	15.2
65–74 years old	18.0
75 years old and above	15.1
Income	
Less than $10,000	1.9
$10,000 to $24,999	7.6
$25,000 to $49,999	14.0
$50,000 to $99,999	25.8
$100,000 and higher	44.8

Note: Excludes money market mutual funds and funds held through retirement accounts or other managed assets.
Source: U.S. Bureau of the Census, *Statistical Abstract of the United States,* Washington, D.C., Government Printing Office, 2001.

Between 1988 and 1998 actively managed, diversified U.S. stock funds returned only 15.6 percent per year compared to the S&P 500's 19.2 percent average annual gain. Furthermore, because of the frequent trading that occurs in actively managed portfolios, investors in actively managed funds typically face higher fees and higher taxes than investors in passively managed funds.

Mutual funds can also be classified by investment objective and by the kind of investment instrument selected to serve various

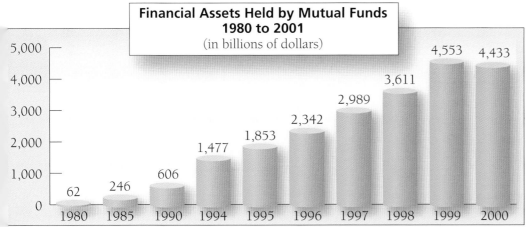

Financial Assets Held by Mutual Funds 1980 to 2001 (in billions of dollars)

Source: U.S. Bureau of the Census, *Statistical Abstract of the United States,* Washington, D.C., Government Printing Office, 2001.

In the 1990s, a boom time for mutual funds, a stockbroker is reflected in the digital board.

objectives. Categories include stock funds, taxable bond funds, municipal bond funds, and stock and bond funds. Within each category, the objective of the fund is broken down further. For example, the stock fund category includes growth stock funds, utility stock funds, and international stock funds.

The Benefits of Mutual Fund Investing

The benefits of mutual fund investing include diversification, ease of use, liquidity (ease of converting mutual fund assets to cash), and professional management. The first two considerations are the most important for beginning investors.

When an individual invests $100 in a mutual fund, she becomes the owner of a certain number of shares of that fund and literally owns a small percentage of every asset that the mutual fund owns. Therefore, she has diversified her $100 investment across several companies rather than putting the entire $100 in the stock of a single company. Diversification is important because it decreases the risk associated with investing and helps to produce more reliable returns. Some experts suggest that investors who purchase individual stocks must have $100,000 in their portfolios to achieve adequate diversification. With mutual funds, each dollar invested is spread across many different companies.

Most individual stocks sell for $10 to $100 per share, and investors cannot initially

buy fractional shares. Therefore, investing small amounts of money in individual stocks is difficult. However, investing small amounts of money in mutual funds is easy because mutual funds do sell fractional shares. Thus, investors can set up investment programs where they automatically invest as little as $50 per month in a mutual fund. If the mutual fund has a NAV of $10.50 per share on the day the $50 investment is made, for example, the investor will purchase 4.76 shares of the fund.

Individual mutual funds use a variety of fee structures. Most funds charge investors an annual fee to cover operating expenses, including fund manager salaries and advertising expenses. Annual fees are usually less than 3 percent. For example, if a fund returns 8 percent during the year and the expense fee is 2 percent, investors realize only 6 percent after annual fees have been deducted. In addition, some funds charge a commission, or front-end load, when the investor purchases the fund; others impose a redemption charge when the investor sells his shares. No-load funds impose no commission charges but may charge higher annual expense fees. Passively managed funds (index funds) are typically no-load funds, and they often have lower annual fees than actively managed funds.

Investors can create a strong portfolio by investing in a group of stock and bond funds with a variety of objectives. Successful investors choose funds with low annual expenses that have consistently performed well over a long period, and they monitor their portfolio at least annually to ensure that all investments remain appropriate to their situation and to the current state of the economy.

Further Reading

Bogle, John C. *Bogle on Mutual Funds: New Perspectives for the Intelligent Investor.* New York: McGraw-Hill, 1993.

Pozen, Robert C. *The Mutual Fund Business.* 2nd ed. New York: Houghton Mifflin, 2002.

Reilly, Frank K., and Edgar A. Norton. *Investments.* 6th ed. Mason, Ohio: Thomson/South-Western, 2003.

Rowland, Mary. *The New Commonsense Guide to Mutual Funds.* Princeton, N.J.: Bloomberg Press, 1998.

—Angeline Lavin

Nader, Ralph

1934–
Activist

Consumer advocate and occasional presidential candidate Ralph Nader is a divisive figure, alternately lauded for helping to launch the consumerist movement and reviled for his strong anticorporate views. His strident criticism of the U.S. economic and political system has led some to view him as a visionary leader; it has led others to deride him as "Saint Ralph," a self-promoting and destructive fanatic.

Born in Winsted, Connecticut, on February 27, 1934, Nader was the youngest of four children in the family of Nathra and Rose Nader, Lebanese immigrants who ran a successful restaurant. Nader's parents were community activists; Nathra was known for discussing politics avidly, even with patrons of his restaurant.

A gifted student in high school, Nader attended Princeton University, where he studied Far Eastern languages and politics. He graduated with honors in 1955 and entered Harvard Law School. At Harvard, Nader worked on a student newspaper that he tried unsuccessfully to make over into a national journal of radical thought. Upon his graduation in 1958, he enlisted in the U.S. Army, primarily to avoid getting drafted, and served for six months as an army cook in Fort Dix, New Jersey.

Nader left the army in 1959 and began practicing law in Connecticut. Being a lawyer did not hold Nader's interest, however, and he soon began writing magazine articles on a variety of subjects, including automobile safety. At the time, the automobile industry was largely self-regulating, and many automobile safety features that are common today were unknown. Nader became increasingly outraged about automobile safety, convinced that manufacturers were sacrificing lives to preserve profits.

In 1964 Nader came to the attention of Daniel Patrick Moynihan, an assistant secretary of labor (and a future senator) who shared Nader's concerns about automobile safety. Moynihan invited Nader to serve as a consultant to the Labor Department. Nader moved to Washington, D.C., where he assisted a Senate subcommittee in planning for hearings on automobile safety.

In 1965 Nader published *Unsafe at Any Speed*, a book that charged the automobile industry with inadequate attention to safety in automobile design. The book pointed to General Motors' Chevrolet Corvair as an example of highly unsafe design. The Corvair tended to flip over. General Motors contended that the car flipped over only when it was driven recklessly; Nader contended that the car was poorly designed and unsafe no matter how carefully people drove it.

At the time of the book's publication, a group of Corvair drivers had sued General Motors, and the automobile manufacturer, suspicious of the coincidence, sought to

See also:
Consumerism; Corporate Social Responsibility; Environmental Regulation; General Motors; Regulation of Business and Industry.

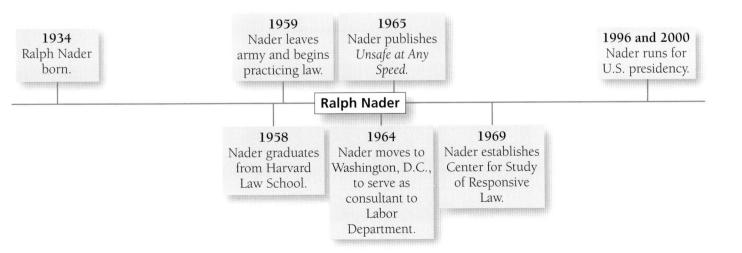

1934
Ralph Nader born.

1959
Nader leaves army and begins practicing law.

1965
Nader publishes *Unsafe at Any Speed.*

1996 and 2000
Nader runs for U.S. presidency.

Ralph Nader

1958
Nader graduates from Harvard Law School.

1964
Nader moves to Washington, D.C., to serve as consultant to Labor Department.

1969
Nader establishes Center for Study of Responsive Law.

discover whether Nader had a financial interest in the lawsuit. In a colossal error of judgment, the company hired private detectives to investigate Nader. The detectives questioned Nader's acquaintances about his sex life and his attitudes toward Jews. Nader reported that in the course of this investigation he received threatening phone calls and was approached by strange women in a salacious manner.

In retrospect, clearly no one could have investigated Nader without his finding out about it. A wary, intensely solitary individual, he lived alone, did not have a full-time job, and did not date. He did not want people to know where he lived, and he warned acquaintances that their phones might be tapped and their offices bugged. He soon learned of the investigation, and he alerted his friends in the Senate and the Johnson

Ralph Nader speaking in 1979 on behalf of a consumer-rights organization he helped found, the Public Citizen.

administration. Officials from General Motors, testifying before the Senate subcommittee investigating auto safety, were then questioned about the case, and in the spotlight of public hearings they were obliged to exonerate Nader and apologize to him. Later that year, President Lyndon Johnson signed a law that placed auto safety under federal oversight.

The resulting publicity made Nader a household name, and he gained considerable wealth from a settlement he obtained after filing an invasion of privacy lawsuit against General Motors. In 1968 Nader turned to organizing "Nader's Raiders," groups of college students who would investigate federal agencies and corporations and publish critical reports. A year later he established the Center for the Study of Responsive Law, the first of more than a dozen groups he would found, including Public Citizen, the Public Interest Research Group, Corporate Accountability Research Group, and the Public Safety Research Institute.

As the names of these groups suggest, Nader's interests reach beyond automobile safety to a range of issues, including food safety and workers' rights. His efforts on behalf of such causes contributed to the passage of new laws to protect workers and consumers in the late 1960s and early 1970s, including the Freedom of Information Act of 1966 and the Clean Air Act of 1970.

Nader himself has dismissed these achievements as insufficient, however. Claiming that abuse of the public interest is inevitable in a system that permits large corporations to exist, he has continued to call for everstricter government regulation of business practices. He has extended his criticisms to politicians and regulatory agencies, charging them with complicity in corporate wrongdoing. His contentions gained Nader a base of support on the political Left, but even there he has proved to be controversial. He has criticized the feminist and gay rights movements, for example, claiming that they ignore the role of large corporations in fostering social injustice.

Corporations always quest for power. They don't just quest for market profits, they quest for power against all forces that might counteract them, whether it's government, law and order, regulatory agencies, whether it's trade unions, whether it's consumer groups. . . . In fact, much of the benefits that have come from corporations in our country's history have flowed precisely because they weren't allowed to follow the logical conclusion of their greed, the logical conclusion of their will to dominate. . . .

We often forget that, because the corporations like to take credit for everything that happens to our economy—it's as if the workers didn't build this economy, as if the slaves didn't build the plantation economy, as if consumers didn't make it by their buying the products. Of course, everybody's involved in building an economy.

But what we must recognize is that in any society—and this goes right back to 2,000 years ago—any society that lets the profit-seeking, mercantile value system dominate other values of humanity—justice, opportunity, health, safety, respect for future generations, the intangibles of civilization—any society that allows the mercantile, the profit-seeking system to dominate gets into trouble. That was described in the Bible, of course, and nothing is very much changed.

—Ralph Nader, speech at St. Francis Church, Sacramento, California, October 17, 1996

Nader's anticorporate stance continues to generate support in some circles. In 1996 Nader ran for president of the United States as the candidate of the Green Party. In 2000 Nader again sought the presidency as the Green Party candidate, winning 3 percent of the nationwide vote, or roughly 2.66 million votes. Although his share of the total votes cast was small, it was enough for some to credit Nader, or blame him, for taking votes away from Democratic candidate Al Gore, thus helping to elect Republican George W. Bush. Not surprisingly, Nader has embraced his role as spoiler, claiming that the Democratic Party has become as much a tool of corporate interests as the Republicans. Also not surprisingly, Nader's critics have charged him with betraying the liberal agenda for his own aggrandizement.

Further Reading

Buckhorn, Robert F. *Nader: The People's Lawyer.* Englewood Cliffs, N.J.: Prentice-Hall, 1972.

Burt, Dan M. *Abuse of Trust: A Report on Ralph Nader's Network.* Chicago: Regnery Gateway, 1982.

Gorey, Hays. *Nader and the Power of Everyman.* New York: Grosset & Dunlap, 1975.

Nader, Ralph. *Unsafe at Any Speed: The Designed-In Dangers of the American Automobile.* Expanded ed. New York: Grossman, 1972.

Whiteside, Thomas. *The Investigation of Ralph Nader: General Motors vs. One Determined Man.* New York: Arbor House, 1972.

—Mary Sisson

See also:

International Trade; North American Free Trade Agreement; Retail and Wholesale.

NAICS Codes

The North American Industry Classification System (NAICS) is a six-digit coding system that was adopted by the U.S. Office of Management and Budget in 1997 to improve classification of the nation's businesses. NAICS (pronounced "nakes") is the result of a joint effort by the United States, Canada, and Mexico. The system is employed by the government to collect data that are used to measure industry productivity, labor costs, and capital intensity and to indicate which kinds of businesses use the goods produced by each economic sector. It also assists individual firms by helping them to identify possible business partners and to estimate the purchase potential of those customers.

NAICS replaced the Standard Industrial Classification (SIC), which was developed in the United States during the 1930s. Although the SIC was regularly revised, critics in the early 1990s complained that the system did not adequately reflect the major changes in the American economy during the last decades of the twentieth century. In addition, the SIC was not intended to be compatible with non–U.S. classification systems. This shortcoming became critical following the 1994 implementation of the North American Free Trade Agreement (NAFTA), which was designed to create a free trade area among Canada, Mexico, and the United States.

Compared with the SIC, NAICS offers a number of advantages. First, by grouping together all economic units that employ similar processes to produce goods and services, the new system uses a single principle to classify businesses and thereby assures the consistency of collected data. Second, NAICS identifies for the first time 358 industries that have developed since the 1980s. The new industries, which include satellite telecommunications, HMO medical centers, management consulting services, fiber-optic cable manufacturing, and diet and weight-loss centers, are varied and reflect the growing importance of technology and of service providers. Third, NAICS permits the development of comparable statistical data among NAFTA partners and makes possible the tracking of cross-border trade flows in North America. It is also similar to the United Nations' International Standard Industrial Classification System (ISCS), which is used throughout Europe and in other parts of the world. Finally, NAICS is scheduled for review every five years. This frequent updating permits the classification system to reflect ongoing changes in the economy.

The NAICS system establishes 20 broad industry sectors, 16 of which are service related. Within the six-digit code, the first two numbers identify a specific industry; for example, 51 relates to the information industry. The third digit specifies an industry subsector, so that 513 is broadcasting and telecommunications. The fourth digit refers to an industry group, for example, 5133 for telecommunications. The fifth digit further refines the classification to identify an NAICS industry; in the current example 51332 represents wireless telecommunications carriers (except satellite). To the five-digit level, Canadian, U.S., and Mexican data are fully comparable. The system also provides a sixth digit, which each of the member countries may or may not use to further subdivide a five-digit category. The United States uses this capacity to differentiate paging with the six-digit code number 513321 from cellular and other wireless telecommunications that are assigned the number 513322. If a country does not opt to add further delineation, the six-digit code ends in zero.

Elements of a NAICS Code

Specific industry · Industry group · Optional further delineation · Industry subsector · NAICS industry

513322

NAICS is a clean-slate classification system. Although a few SIC division titles such as mining, construction, and manufacturing do have the same NAICS sector titles, all lower-level classifications are either new or revised. All NAICS numeric codes are also different from those of the SIC. At the five-digit level, NAICS represents 422 SIC industries without substantial change and classifies another 38 that can be easily traced to SIC counterparts. For those industries, comparability of NAICS and SIC data is relatively straightforward. NAICS, however, redefined 390 industries and established another 320. For those industries NAICS and SIC data are not directly comparable, although sophisticated statistical techniques may allow reasonable estimations with some.

In the United States, implementation of NAICS began with the 1997 Economic Census. Adoption of NAICS by all other governmental agencies is expected around 2004. Canadian implementation of NAICS began with that nation's annual business surveys in 1997 and was largely completed by 2000. With its 1998 Economic Census, Mexico likewise began NAICS implementation.

In 1997 NAICS introduced classification codes for products such as this telecommunications equipment that had been overlooked by the SIC system.

Advantages of NAICS

- Uses single principle for classification, thereby assuring consistency of collected data
- Identifies 358 new industries that reflect the growing importance of technology and service providers in the economy
- Permits development of comparable statistical data among NAFTA partners
- Is similar to the United Nations' International Standard Industrial Classification System used in Europe and elsewhere
- Frequent updates permit the system to reflect changes in the economy

Further Reading

Executive Office of the President, Office of Management and Budget. *North American Industry Classification System: United States, 2002.* Washington, D.C.: Executive Office of the President: Office of Management and Budget, 2002.

U.S. Bureau of the Census. "North American Industry Classification System." http://www.census.gov/naics (October 1, 2002).

—*Marilyn Lavin*

Nasdaq

According to the Securities Industry Association, half of all U.S. households own stock, and young people are one of the fastest-growing groups of new investors. As the number of individuals investing in the stock market has increased, so has the public's familiarity with the market. The Nasdaq, the newest of the three national stock exchanges in the United States, began trading stocks on February 8, 1971. The other exchanges are the New York Stock Exchange (NYSE), which was established in 1796, and the American Stock Exchange (AMEX), which was established in 1910.

Nasdaq stands for National Association of Securities Dealers Automatic Quotation System (the form of the acronym has been changed from NASDAQ to Nasdaq). Defining that phrase requires a little history. Some stocks are not large enough to trade on the NYSE and AMEX. Prior to the creation of the Nasdaq market, smaller stocks traded in the over-the-counter (OTC) market. In 1961 the Securities and Exchange Commission criticized the OTC market for being fragmented and proposed that the market be automated to combat this problem. The Nasdaq Stock Market was the product of this automation process; it was the first electronic-based stock market, designed as an efficient system for storing and displaying quotations on OTC securities. In 1971, 2,500 OTC stocks began trading on the Nasdaq when 500 market makers (the dealers who facilitate trading Nasdaq stocks) were linked by a nationwide computer network. Since 1971 the Nasdaq has evolved into an organized securities market that is distinctly separate from the OTC market.

Market makers are the backbone of Nasdaq trading because they use their own money to maintain an inventory of stocks. Customer orders to buy and sell stocks are submitted to market makers who either purchase the stock for their own inventory, fill the order out of their existing inventory, or buy shares from other market makers to complete the trade. The Nasdaq market is referred to as a dealer market because the market makers actually take possession of the assets that they trade. As a dealer market, the Nasdaq market is fundamentally different from the auction market structure of the NYSE and the AMEX. In auction markets, a broker brings buyers and sellers together, but the broker never takes possession of the asset being traded.

Location and structure are the other major differences between the Nasdaq and the other national markets. Unlike the NYSE and the AMEX, the Nasdaq has no physical location or trading floor. The Nasdaq market uses an "open architecture" market structure with no geographic

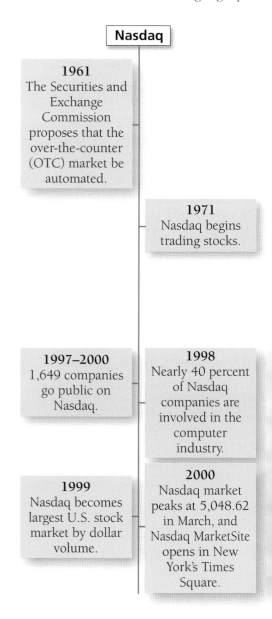

Nasdaq

1961
The Securities and Exchange Commission proposes that the over-the-counter (OTC) market be automated.

1971
Nasdaq begins trading stocks.

1997–2000
1,649 companies go public on Nasdaq.

1998
Nearly 40 percent of Nasdaq companies are involved in the computer industry.

1999
Nasdaq becomes largest U.S. stock market by dollar volume.

2000
Nasdaq market peaks at 5,048.62 in March, and Nasdaq MarketSite opens in New York's Times Square.

boundaries that allows virtually unlimited numbers of market participants to trade a company's stock. Nasdaq market makers are located throughout the United States and execute trades through a sophisticated computer and telecommunications network that is headquartered in Connecticut with a backup in Maryland. The computer network transmits trade data and real-time quotes to more than 1.3 million users in 83 countries. Although Nasdaq trading takes place throughout the United States, the public can visit the Nasdaq MarketSite, which opened in 2000 in Times Square in New York City.

The Nasdaq market is the fastest growing major stock market in the world. Approximately 6,400 innovative, emerging company stocks in fast-growing industries like information technology and biotechnology trade on the Nasdaq market. The companies that trade on the Nasdaq are divided into two groups. The Nasdaq National Market includes about 5,000 national and international companies while the Nasdaq SmallCap Market includes the remaining 1,400 companies. The stocks that trade on the Nasdaq National Market tend to be larger companies with more shares outstanding and a longer business history. Many well-known companies trade on the Nasdaq including Microsoft, Intel, Amgen, Northwest Airlines, and Cisco. As of 1998 nearly 40 percent of all Nasdaq companies were involved with the computer industry, 29 percent were industrials, 14 percent were finance companies, and 12 percent were telecommunications firms.

The Nasdaq Composite Index is often used to summarize ups and downs in the Nasdaq market. The Nasdaq Composite Index measures the market value of all domestic and foreign common stocks listed on the Nasdaq Stock Market. From 1990 to 1999 the average annual return on the Nasdaq Composite index was 24.5 percent compared to the S&P 500's average annual return of 18.20 percent. The difference in performance of the two measures is attributable to the different kinds of companies

that each index tracks. The S&P 500 tracks the performance of 500 of the largest firms in the United States while the Nasdaq Composite tracks technology stocks, including dot-com firms. This difference in composition explains the Nasdaq market's tumble that began in 2000. The Nasdaq market peaked at 5,048.62 on March 10, 2000, but by the end of April 2000, the

The Nasdaq display room in 1998; the Nasdaq composite screens show up-to-date gains and losses.

The Manhattan offices of Nasdaq in 2002.

Nasdaq was down 23.5 percent from this high. For the entire year 2000, the Nasdaq Composite was down 40 percent, and it continued that trend with a 15 percent decline in 2001.

In 1999 the Nasdaq Stock Market became the largest U.S. stock market by dollar volume. The Nasdaq has repeatedly broken records for the number of shares traded on a particular trading day and frequently reaches trading volumes of more than two billion shares per day. To prepare for the future, the Nasdaq increased its trading capacity tenfold between 1997 and 2002. The Nasdaq is now capable of trading six billion shares per day. Between 1997 and 2000, 1,649 companies were brought public on the Nasdaq. Through this process, over

$3 billion was raised for the companies, and thousands of jobs were added to the American economy. More than any other exchange, the Nasdaq market continues to be the engine for capital formation and job creation in the United States.

Further Reading

Gitman, Lawrence J., and Michael D. Joehnk. *Fundamentals of Investing.* 8th ed. New York: Addison-Wesley, 2002.

Ingebretsen, Mark. *Nasdaq: A History of the Market That Changed the World.* Roseville, Calif.: Forum, 2002.

Isaacman, Max. *The Nasdaq Investor.* New York: McGraw-Hill, 2001.

Nasdaq Backgrounder. *The Nasdaq Stock Market.* Washington, D.C.: Nasdaq Backgrounder, 1998.

—*Angeline Lavin*

National Black Chamber of Commerce

The National Black Chamber of Commerce (NBCC) was established in Washington, D.C., in March 1993 as the successor organization to the National Negro Business League (NNBL). It serves as an advocacy forum for 64,000 black-owned businesses throughout the United States.

The NNBL was established by Booker T. Washington, founder and first president of the historically black Tuskegee Institute, in 1900. The NNBL encouraged the development of African American businesses at that time. The idea for the organization emerged at the Fourth Atlanta University Conference, held in Atlanta, Georgia, in 1898. Resolutions were passed that proclaimed that black business enterprise should be substantially expanded and that African Americans should become their own producers and employers to achieve economic independence.

Based on Washington's philosophy of self-help, honesty, and thrift, the NNBL sought to facilitate economic advancement. Supported by white captains of industry of the period, including John D. Rockefeller, Andrew Carnegie, and others, its goal was to develop local black businesses, provide them with business planning advice and technical and management assistance, and to assist them in gaining access to business capital. The NNBL encouraged and supported grocery stores, drugstores, restaurants, lumber mills, cemeteries, mortuaries, beauty and barbershops, banks, and a host of other small- and medium-sized businesses in the early twentieth century. By 1907 the NNBL had 320 branches across the nation with more than 30,000 members. However, by

See also:
Affirmative Action;
Professional Associations;
Small Business
Administration.

An 1899 photo of the board of directors of Coleman Co., then the only black-owned cotton mill in the United States.

1970, membership had declined to 13,000 in 72 chapters.

The National Black Chamber of Commerce (NBCC), a nonprofit, nonpartisan, nonsectarian organization whose mission is the economic empowerment of African American communities, has 190 affiliated chapters throughout the United States and international affiliate chapters in the Bahamas, Brazil, Colombia, Ghana, and Jamaica. The NBCC's mission largely paralleled that of the National Negro Business League in providing management training and technical assistance. Unlike the NNBL, the NBCC focuses heavily on government programs for minority, disadvantaged, and women-owned businesses. With the growth of federal, state, and local government-sponsored programs for such businesses since the 1970s, the NBCC has directed its black enterprise initiatives through government-funded programs. Moreover, several of its executives and managers have previously held appointments in the federal Small Business Administration (SBA), and its local chapters are substantially engaged in programs with regional units of the SBA.

The NBCC was heavily involved in the drafting of the Clinton administration's New Markets Initiatives in the late 1990s; these initiatives are designed to stimulate investment in the nation's socially and economically distressed urban and rural areas. This legislation authorizes the SBA to guarantee up to $150 million in loans to match $100 million in private equity and to make $30 million in grants for operating assistance to new market venture capital firms (NMVC). The New Market Initiatives also include an affordable lending program to increase home ownership within low-income minority communities with the goal of adding one million homeowners by 2005 and incentives for job development in low-employment communities.

The NBCC's goal of economic empowerment for the African American community is broad in scope—ranging from the development of human, social, and cultural capital to business development. Its strategy encompasses both social welfare and business; the NBCC gives as much attention to

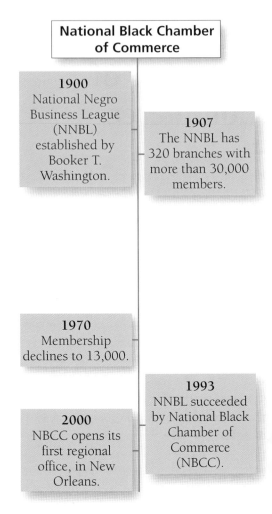

National Black Chamber of Commerce

1900
National Negro Business League (NNBL) established by Booker T. Washington.

1907
The NNBL has 320 branches with more than 30,000 members.

1970
Membership declines to 13,000.

1993
NNBL succeeded by National Black Chamber of Commerce (NBCC).

2000
NBCC opens its first regional office, in New Orleans.

job acquisition for African Americans in corporate America as it does to the establishment of African American businesses. The NBCC's multiple goals of developing an employee base, a customer base, and an entrepreneurial base in the overall revitalization of distressed black communities may conflict with the general profit motives of both minority and majority businesses. The nagging question is whether social-welfare and business-oriented approaches can be successfully combined under the NBCC umbrella of economic empowerment for African American communities.

Further Reading

Franklin, J. H., and A. A. Moss. *From Slavery to Freedom.* 8th ed. New York: Alfred A. Knopf, 2000.

The National Black Chamber of Commerce. http://www.nationalbcc.org (February 24, 2003).

—*Walter C. Farrell, Jr., Reneé Sartin Kirby, and Douglas Bynum*

National Education Association

The National Education Association (NEA) is the largest and oldest labor union for public school teachers (and other education employees) in the United States. Its members support local affiliates in all 50 states, as well as state and national offices. State and national staff members of the NEA are the major group that lobbies state legislatures and the U.S. Congress about education issues.

The Early Years

Building on the work of local and state educators who had begun to organize teachers as professionals throughout the early 1850s, the national association was founded after the presidents of 10 state associations—Illinois, Indiana, Iowa, Massachusetts, Missouri, New Hampshire, New York, Pennsylvania, Vermont, and Wisconsin—called for a meeting of interested teachers in 1857.

Under the leadership of Daniel B. Hagar of Massachusetts and Thomas W. Valentine of New York, 43 teachers met in Philadelphia to form the National Teachers' Association (NTA). The purposes of the new organization were stated in its constitution: "To elevate the character and advance the interests of the profession of teaching, and to promote the cause of popular education in the United States." Membership in the association was limited to "gentlemen," although two of the original signatories were female honorary members. Women were not admitted as full members until 1866. The first female president of the NEA, Ella Flagg Young, was elected in 1910. Despite this late start, the NEA ardently supported equal rights for women, both within the profession and in American society at large.

The NTA (which become the NEA in 1870 after mergers with the American Normal School Association and the National Association of School Superintendents) was formed at a time of growth and change in American education. Each of the states that sent delegates to the 1857 meeting in Philadelphia had recently passed laws that called for the construction and staffing of a

See also:
Collective Bargaining; Education Industry; National Labor Relations Act; Women in the Workforce.

In one-room schoolhouses like this one in Breathitt County, Kentucky, all grades were taught in the same room.

variety of public school systems. This common school movement was a reaction to the dearth of educational opportunities for American children before the 1840s. Only children of the very wealthy were able to acquire adequate educations by attending the private college academies or by traveling to boarding schools in New England or in Europe. Faced in the late 1840s and 1850s with a growing number of undereducated and increasingly delinquent children in the cities of the Northeast and Midwest, the various state legislatures mandated the organization and financing of entire school systems by municipal governments.

With these laws came a multitude of local and state education bureaucracies that controlled the education systems. Young teachers, many of whom had little education themselves, were hired to staff the new schools. Therefore, in 1857 when the NEA was founded, the overwhelming majority of teachers across the nation were under 25 years of age and most of them had taught for less than five years. Most of the teachers were men, but there was a de facto segregation by gender and by grade: the primary grades were increasingly staffed by female teachers while most of the high school teaching positions were held by men. The founding teachers of the NEA in Philadelphia were concerned about the future of their profession. American educators were forging a new path, and teachers were concerned that their interests and those of their students were not being protected.

From its founding in 1857, the NEA allowed African American membership. However, in some states, black teachers could not join the white local and state associations. The national organization allowed for separate black- and white-affiliated associations in 18 states and the District of Columbia until the 1960s. In 1904 African American teachers formed the American Teachers Association (ATA). The NEA and the ATA cooperated to improve conditions in black segregated schools during the first half of the twentieth century. After the 1954 Supreme Court decision *Brown v. Board of Education*, which struck down the "separate but equal" doctrine of segregation, the NEA worked diligently for combined educational rights of African American teachers and children. The ATA and the NEA merged to form the modern NEA in 1966.

The Modern NEA

During its first 50 years, the NEA tackled problems of curriculum reform, including citizenship education and health education. Members also cooperated with textbook publishers, school furniture manufacturers, and classroom supplies dealers to keep schools current with changing expectations and standards. Members of the NEA supported the institutionalization of kindergarten classes, the coeducation of male and female students in American classrooms and in schools for teacher training, and the implementation of the "learning by doing" method of instruction during the late nineteenth and early twentieth centuries. However, the organization also supported, during the same period, a national university that would never come to be, a movement to simplify American spelling that never got off the ground, and an anti-alcohol temperance movement that persuaded few to take the pledge against alcoholic beverages.

American Federation of Teachers and the AFL-CIO

The Teachers' International Union of America was founded in 1916 by reform-minded members of the National Education Association. Today, the AFL-CIO–affiliated public teachers union is the chief rival of the NEA. The original members (from locales including Chicago; New York; Gary, Indiana; Scranton, Pennsylvania; and Washington, D.C.) created the organization to represent classroom teachers exclusively; they viewed the NEA as overly representative of supervisory personnel, who dominated the parent organization. Within three days, the new union's president, Charles B. Stillman, had applied to the American Federation of Labor (AFL) for membership. Samuel Gompers, president of the AFL, granted the charter to the teachers but suggested its name be changed to the American Federation of Teachers (AFT).

From its beginnings within the NEA, the AFT has been identified with the organized labor movement. Its membership is strongest in the nation's larger cities where large numbers of industrial laborers had also organized. Its structure is based on strong local affiliates and relatively weak state ones. The AFT has a long tradition of collective bargaining and lobbying on education legislation. The AFT currently cooperates with the NEA in fighting school privatization and government school voucher programs.

Throughout the NEA's history, individual members were appointed to various committees, commissions, and councils that were charged with researching issues and reporting back to the general membership. For example, the Legislative Commission, established in 1920, worked to persuade legislators to form a national Department of Education. To further the professional interests of NEA members, the committees often met with government officials and corporate executives outside of the educational community. The work performed by staff members for these committees was the predecessor of that of organized lobbyists who work for the contemporary NEA. Committees have also addressed the issues of full funding for local schools from the states, teachers' salaries, and school vouchers. Before the last quarter of the twentieth century, lobbying was restricted to matters that directly affected members. Not until 1976 did the NEA's representative assembly officially endorse candidates for national offices, supporting Jimmy Carter in his presidential campaign.

Beginning in the late nineteenth century, the NEA advocated for salaries that matched a teacher's professional status. Before the 1970s, however, the NEA's role was limited to supporting local affiliates that negotiated with local school boards;

In 1998 National Education Association representatives speak in front of the Florida capitol building in Tallahassee, displaying more than 400,000 petitions in favor of increasing education's share of the Florida budget.

Contemporary Issues of Importance to the NEA

- **Accountability** Believes schools, teachers, policy makers, and parents share accountability for helping every student succeed
- **Charter Schools** Supports public charter schools that have the same standards of accountability and access as other public schools
- **Class Size** Backs reducing class size
- **National Board Certification** Supports voluntary national certification program
- **Privatization** Strongly opposes privatization
- **Low-performing Schools** Works to make improvements in struggling schools a "high priority"
- **School Safety** Advocates using both "hard responses" like metal detectors and "soft responses" like conflict-resolution programs to increase school safety
- **Teacher Quality** Is committed to increasing quality in both beginning and experienced teachers
- **Teacher Shortage** Works to increase teacher pay and improve conditions needed to retain teachers
- **Vouchers** Opposes the use of private school vouchers

the 1935 National Labor Relations Act (NLRA), which applied only to private sector employees, had been slowly reinterpreted during the 1960s to allow states to negotiate with all employees, including teachers. Such negotiations required the holding of collective bargaining elections to determine the rights of exclusive recognition; teachers were asked whether they wanted the NEA or any other organizations (particularly the American Federation of Teachers [AFT], an AFL-CIO affiliate organization) to represent them.

Collective bargaining laws also required the separation of the NEA into represented and nonrepresented members; the result was the division of the association into members who were employees (teachers, support staff) and those who were administrators (principals, superintendents). The support of collective bargaining by the NEA has led to the increased unionization of the organization. A new constitution, ratified by the representative assembly in 1973, guaranteed that teachers would be more dominant in the association than would administrators. The NEA has cooperated with other education organizations and unions, particularly the AFT, in lobbying for the welfare of its members. Attempts have been made to merge the NEA and the AFT since the early 1970s, but all, including the merger vote taken at the representative assembly in 1998, have failed.

The modern National Education Association is recognized as the most important representative body for American schoolteachers. The association's 2.7 million members continue to support the NEA's efforts to protect the important legacy of the nation's public schools. The organization's professional legislative lobbyists have worked to increase federal funding for public schools, to hire more teachers, decrease class size, and to modernize classroom technologies. The NEA has also supported congressional efforts to control the access and sale of firearms (particularly in the wake of numerous incidents of school violence). The organization's members have adamantly opposed education savings accounts and school voucher programs, arguing that they would harm public education efforts by favoring private over public schools, as well as merit pay plans that are based upon subjective administrative judgments rather than upon objective performance standards.

Further Reading

Berube, Maurice R. *Teacher Politics: The Influence of Unions.* New York: Greenwood Press, 1988.

Schultz, Michael John, Jr. *The National Education Association and the Black Teacher: The Integration of a Professional Organization.* Coral Gables, Fla.: University of Miami Press, 1970.

West, Allan M. *The National Education Association: The Power Base for Education.* New York: The Free Press, 1980.

—*Kay J. Car*

National Labor Relations Act

Signed into law in July 1935 by President Franklin Delano Roosevelt, the National Labor Relations Act (NLRA) is considered a high point in the history of the U.S. labor movement. Although greatly amended in subsequent decades, at the time of its passage the NLRA was a sweeping piece of legislation that drastically changed the relationship of labor and management by regulating collective bargaining between employers and employees.

One of the major reform statutes of the New Deal, the NLRA is also known as the Wagner Act, named after its principal author, Senator Robert F. Wagner, Sr., of New York. The law granted workers the right to organize, to determine by majority vote their preferred "bargaining unit" (for example, the company as a whole, or a particular craft or plant unit) and to hold elections to determine their representatives. The law stipulated that such voting was to be carried out without interference, harassment, or coercion from management and required employers to collectively bargain with the representatives elected. Administration of the act was entrusted to the National Labor Relations Board, a three-member board of presidential appointees created to administer union representation elections and to consider complaints of unfair labor practices.

Although the passage of the act was historic, its success was facilitated by the passage of the Norris–La Guardia Act of 1932. This act outlawed two antilabor weapons: the injunction (a decree granted by a judge requiring a person or group to act or cease to act in a specific way, often used to quash labor disputes) and the Yellow-Dog Contract

See also:
Great Depression;
Labor Union; New Deal;
Taft–Hartley Act.

In Pittsburgh in 1937, officials from the National Labor Relations Board watch as workers of the Jones and Laughlin mill vote on whether the Steel Workers Organizing Committee will be their sole bargaining agent.

Key Provisions of the National Labor Relations Act

Created National Labor Relations Board (NLRB)

- To supervise elections to determine appropriate collective bargaining units
- To certify appropriately chosen unions
- To stop unfair practices by employers, employees, or unions
- Upholds right of employees to join unions and bargain collectively through representatives of their own choosing
- Prohibits employers from interfering with union organizing activities
- Protects employees who take part in protests, picketing, or strikes
- Defines unfair labor practices of the employer
  - Interference or coercion directed against union or collective activity
  - Domination of the union administration
  - Discrimination against employees taking part in union activities
  - Retaliation against employees who file charges with the NLRB
  - Refusal to bargain in good faith

The NLRA contained many provisions that strengthened the hand of the labor movement.

(a written agreement that prohibited workers from becoming involved in union activities). The NLRA was essentially a reincarnation of Section 7(a) of the National Industrial Recovery Act (NIRA), which became law in June 1933 but was declared unconstitutional by the Supreme Court in May 1935, along with its administrating agency, the National Recovery Administration.

The NLRA became law during the Great Depression, a time of high and chronic unemployment and economic hardship. Despite a flurry of union recruitment and grandstanding when the NIRA had been passed two years earlier, that law was full of loopholes and was at times completely ignored by industry. Between 1933 and 1935 strikes became more common. "I do not mind telling you," AFL president William Green testified before a congressional committee, "that the spirit of the workers in America had been aroused. They are going to find a way to bargain collectively. . . . We cannot and will not continue to urge workers to have patience, unless the Wagner bill is made law and unless it is enforced once it becomes law."

At the time of its passage the NLRA had widespread support, with public opinion sympathetic to the aspirations of the labor movement. However, the business community was critical of the NLRA, predicting union irresponsibility under its provisions, and expressing general alarm at what it considered a threat to management's control. Some industry leaders ignored the act's provisions altogether, claiming that the NLRA went beyond the power of Congress to regulate interstate commerce and was therefore unconstitutional.

In 1937 the Supreme Court ruled in a series of decisions that the NLRA was constitutional; the most important case was *National Labor Relations Board v. Jones and Laughlin Steel Company.* "Employees have as clear a right to organize and select their representatives for lawful purposes as the respondent has to organize its business and select its own officers and agents," wrote Chief Justice Charles Evan Hughes.

Over the next decade, however, the prolabor sentiment of the New Deal era waned, and antiunion sentiments began to dominate public opinion. Many began to think that the NLRA had granted unions too much power and had enabled organized labor to dominate the economy. In 1947 the NLRA was amended by the Labor–Management Relations Act, commonly known as the Taft–Hartley Act, which placed many restrictions on union activity.

Further Reading

Dubofsky, Melvyn, and Foster Rhea Dulles. *Labor in America: A History.* 6th ed. Wheeling, Ill.: Harlan Davidson, 1999.
Eliot, Thomas H. *Recollections of the New Deal.* Boston: Northeastern University Press, 1992.

—*Barbara Gerber*

New Deal

The term *New Deal* refers to legislation and programs initiated between 1933 and 1938 to promote the recovery of the U.S. economy from the Great Depression. Led by President Franklin Delano Roosevelt (FDR), the federal government expanded its regulation of banks, transportation, securities traders, and communications, and it acknowledged responsibility for the health, well-being, and security of all its citizenry. The New Deal, which preserved the nation's capitalist economic system, relieved the worst human suffering of the Depression. Although it did not bring about lasting economic recovery, the New Deal strengthened the role of government in promoting economic prosperity and established the outline of modern welfare state capitalism.

When Roosevelt assumed the presidency on March 4, 1933, one-quarter of the U.S. labor force was unemployed, banks on the brink of failure were closed in 38 states, and many farmers faced foreclosure. Three years of hard times and ongoing revelations of corruption had discredited the nation's business community.

One day after his inauguration, Roosevelt declared a bank holiday that closed the nation's banks. On March 9, Congress approved and the president signed the Emergency Banking Relief Act that provided for government supervision and assistance to the banks. Four days later, after FDR's first fireside radio chat in which he informed the nation that the government would assure bank solvency, banks began to reopen. The Glass–Steagall Act of June 1933 further strengthened the security of the nation's banks by separating commercial and investment banking and by creating the Federal Deposit Insurance Corporation to insure bank deposits

Early in Roosevelt's presidency, the National Recovery Administration (NRA) promoted planning and cooperation among government, business, and labor through voluntary industry codes. Although the Supreme Court declared the NRA unconstitutional in 1935, Section 7a of the enabling legislation that established the NRA is notable as the first federal recognition of labor's right to bargain collectively. Another early New Deal agency, the Agricultural Adjustment Administration, attempted to raise the prices of agricultural products by subsidizing farmers for taking land out of cultivation. Although it was also ruled unconstitutional, acreage allotments and federal subsidies designed to curtail overproduction continue to be hallmarks of U.S. farm policy.

The most innovative New Deal legislation established the Tennessee Valley Authority (TVA). This effort in regional, long-range planning was responsible for the construction of dams that controlled flooding in seven states along the Tennessee River and provided inexpensive hydroelectric power to the area. The TVA made possible the electrification of an impoverished region and advanced reforestation and conservation programs in the area.

During the early years of the New Deal, a number of agencies attempted to meet the needs of the nation's unemployed. The Federal Emergency Relief Administration provided relief payments to needy citizens; the Civilian Conservation Corps put two million young men to work on environmental projects; the Public Works Administration (PWA) spent

See also:
Fair Labor Standards Act;
Great Depression; National
Labor Relations Act;
Securities and Exchange
Commission; Social Security
and Medicare.

Key New Deal Agencies	
1933	Agricultural Adjustment Administration (AAA)
	Civil Works Administration (CWA)
	Civilian Conservation Corps (CCC)
	Federal Deposit Insurance Corporation (FDIC)
	Federal Emergency Relief Administration (FERA)
	Home Owners Loan Corporation (HOLC)
	National Recovery Administration (NRA)
	Public Works Administration (PWA)
	Tennessee Valley Authority (TVA)
1934	Federal Communications Commission (FCC)
	Federal Housing Administration (FHA)
	Securities and Exchange Commission (SEC)
1935	National Labor Relations Board (NLRB)
	National Youth Administration (NYA)
	Resettlement Administration (RA)
	Rural Electrification Administration (REA)
	Works Progress Administration (WPA)

more than $6 billion on job-creation projects; and the Works Progress Administration (WPA) oversaw a massive relief program designed to put as many people to work as possible. Those efforts eased the immediate suffering of the unemployed, but they did not have lasting impact. By contrast, the Social Security Act of 1935—which guaranteed retirement payments to enrolled workers, set up a federal–state system of unemployment insurance,

A poster advertising a Works Progress Administration art show in 1935.

Texas farmers pick up their benefit checks in 1934.

and established payments to the blind, to the handicapped, and to dependent children—has continued to the present.

New Deal legislation expanded the regulatory powers of the federal government. Despite objections from the business community, the Securities Exchange Act became law in 1934. The act established the Securities and Exchange Commission, placed the trading of securities under federal regulation, and required the registration and disclosure of information about securities traded on exchanges. The Federal Communications Commission (FCC) was created in 1934. The establishment of the FCC, which was charged with regulation of wired and wireless communications, recognized the growing importance of radio in the lives of Americans during the 1930s.

The National Labor Relations Act of 1935 (also known as the Wagner Act) created the National Labor Relations Board to oversee labor–management relations and advanced the right of unions to bargain collectively. The act revitalized the American labor movement and solidified labor support for the Democratic Party. The Fair Labor Standards Act of 1938 further improved the lot of workers by establishing a minimum wage of 40 cents per hour and a maximum workweek of 40 hours.

The New Deal offered modest assistance to African Americans. Most black Americans did not hold the kinds of jobs that would allow them to benefit from labor or social security legislation. However, PWA and WPA relief programs helped the many blacks who migrated to northern cities during the 1930s. African Americans also responded to Roosevelt's pledge that there would be "no . . . forgotten races" in his administration and with the 1936 presidential election shifted their support to the Democrats.

Faced with a nation in crisis, the New Deal sought reform rather than revolution. Roosevelt's administration targeted for greater regulation those areas of the U.S. economy—especially banking, public utilities, and agriculture—that had failed during the late 1920s, but, excepting the TVA, it attempted no grand experiments. The New Deal did, however, initiate lasting changes in the role of the federal government by recognizing government's responsibility to guarantee the welfare of citizens and by bringing the relationship between organized labor and corporate powers into more equal balance. By so doing, the New Deal changed Americans' conception of government and led them to hold government more responsible for helping people who could not help themselves.

Further Reading

Brinkley, Alan. *The End of Reform.* New York: Alfred A. Knopf, 1995.

Leuchtenburg, William. *Franklin D. Roosevelt and the New Deal.* New York: Harper & Row, 1963.

McElvaine, Robert. *The Great Depression: America, 1929–1941.* New York: Times Books, 1984.

—*Marilyn Lavin*

See also:
Ben & Jerry's Homemade;
Corporate Social Responsibility.

Newman's Own

For some businesspeople, making money is comparatively easy, giving it away nearly impossible. For movie star, philanthropist, and businessman Paul Newman, giving money away has always been the easy part.

Paul Newman became famous as an actor, starring in films like *Hud* (1961), *Butch Cassidy and the Sundance Kid* (1969), and *The Verdict* (1982). For many years, Newman and his long-time friend A. E. Hotchner had given wine bottles filled with homemade salad dressing as Christmas gifts. When friends began requesting more of the dressing, Newman and Hotchner decided to start a company as a lark. They established the company in 1982 with 2,000 bottles of vinaigrette dressing and ran the business out of a small office furnished with the Newman family's pool furniture.

At first, Newman was reluctant to use his famous face to sell a commercial product. When a colleague finally convinced him that he would not be able to sell one bottle until he put his face on the label, Newman decided that all of the profits would have to go to charity. "To make money off that would be so tacky," he noted.

Newman eschewed costly market research and ignored industry wisdom that new product launches initially lose substantial sums. He also ignored industry wisdom that preservatives and additives are necessary. Relying on informal taste tests with family and friends, a modest initial investment of $40,000 of his own money, and his famous name, Newman's Own grossed about $3.2 million in sales during its first year.

Newman's Own is a unique business. One hundred percent of the company's after-tax profits are given to the nonprofit Paul Newman Foundation, which, in turn, gives the money to charities. Although the company itself exists to make money, that is only so it will have more money to give away. The entire corporate strategy is based on its charitable purpose.

When he started the company, Newman had a sign over his desk that read, "If we ever have a plan, we're screwed." However, the company grew so quickly that professional management was soon a necessity. Said Newman, "We had come to a juncture where we had to admit that we really shouldn't be running a $60 million company without help." Professional sales and marketing managers were brought in to boost sales and run the company, leaving Newman free to devote more of his time to the foundation and to his film career.

Some of the company's profits were used to establish the Hole in the Wall Gang Camps in 1986. These international camps allow seriously and terminally ill children to experience camping and the outdoors. The camps are now independent from the Newman Foundation and receive donations from many other philanthropic

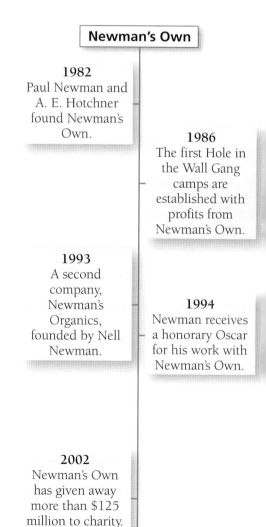

Newman's Own

1982
Paul Newman and A. E. Hotchner found Newman's Own.

1986
The first Hole in the Wall Gang camps are established with profits from Newman's Own.

1993
A second company, Newman's Organics, founded by Nell Newman.

1994
Newman receives a honorary Oscar for his work with Newman's Own.

2002
Newman's Own has given away more than $125 million to charity.

Paul Newman pours some of his Newman's Own salad dressing over the head of TV host Gary Chapman during the taping of the cable TV show Prime Time Country *in Nashville in 1997.*

organizations. Today, Newman's Own contributes to more than 1,000 nonprofit organizations around the world. All of the money is used to help finance programs in countries where Newman's Own products are sold. While supporting major organizations, the Paul Newman Foundation also gives to smaller, lesser-known charities that may lack the cachet to attract other corporate donors.

The charities to which Newman's Own donates are varied, including causes like the Scott Newman Foundation for drug and alcohol abuse education (named for Newman's son who died of an overdose),

drought relief in Africa, children's charities, health charities, and charities involved in education, medical care, and helping the needy, the homeless, and the environment. Organizations apply to the foundation representative in their home country. To qualify for aid, charities must receive minimal government funding, spend their grants within the country they operate in, spend the grant on a particular project, and not use grant monies to fund salaries or administrative costs. Submissions that fulfill these criteria are forwarded to Newman and his business partner, Ursula Gwynne, who make the final decisions. As Newman

In 1999 Paul Newman addresses a meeting of business leaders on the subject of corporate philanthropy.

says, "That's what makes this business such a kick—the mutually beneficial recycling from the haves to the have-nots."

In the interest of survival, Newman is a recent, and reluctant, convert to the concept of "noisy philanthropy." When research indicated that most consumers were unaware that Newman's Own donated all after-tax profits to charity, Newman became more vocal about his company's good deeds. He has also joined with several other business leaders, including John Whitehead, Paul Volcker, David Rockefeller, and Ben Cohen of Ben and Jerry's Homemade, to create a nonprofit business center to promote corporate philanthropy.

By early 2002 Newman's Own had given away more than $125 million in profits from the sale of salad dressing, pasta sauce, salsa, popcorn, steak sauce, ice cream, and lemonade. Newman's Own has also engendered a second company, Newman's Organics, founded in 1993 by Newman's daughter Nell Newman. Newman's Organics concentrates on all-organic products and, like the parent company, all after-tax profits go to the Paul Newman Foundation.

Paul Newman believes that businesses have a responsibility to give money back to the communities in which they operate, and that businesses can best help themselves and encourage growth by engaging in socially responsible practices. Although acknowledging that most companies cannot afford to give away all of their profits, Newman hopes that Newman's Own can be used as a model. "Government has become less involved in its social responsibilities, and to a great extent it is the business sector that has encouraged this move toward less government. I believe it is only right that those businesses should assume a greater role in giving back to social causes." In 1994 Newman was awarded his second Oscar—this time it was the Jean Hersholt Humanitarian Award for his work with Newman's Own.

Further Reading

Quirk, Lawrence J. *Paul Newman: The Man Behind the Steel Blue Eyes*. Petersburg, Fla.: Taylor Publishing, 1997.

Rafferty, Renata J. *Don't Just Give It Away: How to Make the Most of Your Charitable Giving*. Madison, W.I.: Chandler House Press, 1999.

Weeden, Curt. *Corporate Social Investing: New Strategies for Giving and Getting Corporate Contributions*. San Francisco, Calif.: Berrett-Koehler, 1998.

—*Lisa Magloff*

New York Stock Exchange

Established in 1792 by a group of 24 merchants, the New York Stock Exchange (NYSE) is the oldest national exchange in the United States. Originally the merchants met under a tree at what is now 68 Wall Street to trade stocks, bonds, and commodities, and they laid the foundation for the "Big Board." The organization became known as the New York Stock Exchange in 1817 when the brokers rented space on Wall Street and formally established trading rules. Initially, trading volume was low, and the first 100-share day did not occur until the 1820s. Even the quoting of prices in the early days of the NYSE was difficult; the earliest price postings were on chalkboards in taverns across the street from the exchange.

However, the exchange continued and grew along with the American capitalist system. As the United States became more industrialized, the number of stocks traded on the exchange increased. The first real-time price ticker was introduced in 1867, and the first one-million-share day occurred in 1886. As more Americans became interested in owning shares of stock, the need for information about the markets grew. In 1896 Charles Dow developed a daily average that tracked the 12 leading stocks on the NYSE, thus giving investors a benchmark for their equity investments.

The ups and downs of the NYSE have paralleled U.S. history. In July 1914 the world was on the brink of World War I, and stock markets around the globe began to close their doors. On July 31, 1914, the NYSE closed and did not reopen until December 15, 1914. A bull market (period of rising prices) followed World War I, ending with the crash of 1929 and the ensuing Great Depression. World War II helped to create another bull market in the 1940s, but the market did not surpass its 1929 high until 1954. In 1973–1974, the U.S. economy experienced one of the worst recessions in its history, and the market suffered accordingly. After the high inflation of the late 1970s passed, market conditions improved, and 1982 marked the beginning of one of the longest bull markets in U.S. history. Despite a short but significant downturn in 1987, the bull

See also:
Dow Jones Averages;
Investment; Nasdaq; Stocks
and Bonds.

New York Stock Exchange

1792
Group of 24 merchants forms stock exchange.

1817
New York Stock Exchange (NYSE) established; brokers formally set trading rules.

1867
First real-time price ticker introduced.

1896
Charles Dow develops daily average to track the 12 leading stocks on the NYSE.

1914
NYSE closes from July 31 until December 15 due to World War I.

1929
Stock market crash ends bull market.

1954
Market surpasses 1929 high.

1973–1974
Market suffers during recession.

1982–2000
One of the longest bull markets in U.S. history.

Daily Shares Traded 1900 to 2000
(in thousands)

Year	Daily Average	Record High	Record Low
1900	505	1,627	89
1910	601	1,656	111
1920	828	2,008	227
1930	2,959	8,279	1,090
1940	751	3,940	130
1950	1,980	4,859	1,061
1960	2,578	7,717	1,230
1965	3,042	5,303	1,894
1970	6,176	11,434	3,028
1980	44,871	8,4297	16,132
1985	109,169	181,027	62,055
1990	156,777	292,364	56,853
1995	346,101	652,829	117,723
1998	673,590	1,216,326	246,928
1999	809,183	1,349,711	312,093
2000	1,041,578	1,560,808	403,254

Source: New York Stock Exchange, *Fact Book: 2000*, 2001.

market that began in 1982 did not end until 2000.

The exchange currently lists the stock of more than 2,800 firms. The stock of domestic companies comprises most of the daily trading volume on the NYSE, although the exchange does trade the stock of about 400 foreign firms as well as options on stock, corporate bonds, and closed-end mutual funds. The NYSE is structured as an auction market: all orders to buy and sell shares on the NYSE ultimately come together at one central location, on the trading floor at 18 Broad Street in lower Manhattan. The floor of the NYSE has 1,366 members who participate in trading. Members own "seats," which confer trading privileges. Most members are employed by brokerage firms to trade for the firm; however, a few independent brokers own their seats. In 2001 a seat on the exchange cost between $1.5 and $2 million.

Specialists, the backbone of NYSE trading, are charged with maintaining a fair and orderly market. Approximately 450 exchange members are specialists; they help facilitate the process of matching customer buy and sell orders and sometimes purchase shares for their own accounts. The specialists of the NYSE do not always take possession of the assets that are traded. As an auction market, the NYSE differs fundamentally from the dealer market structure of the Nasdaq, where the traders usually take possession of the assets that they trade.

The NYSE has requirements that a company must meet before it can be listed on the exchange. These requirements pertain to items like pretax income, tangible assets, market value of the stock, and the number of investors owning at least 100 shares. These listing requirements ensure that stocks listed on the NYSE are of interest to the investment community; adherence to these requirements has sustained the NYSE's reputation as an exchange that is home to high-quality, blue chip companies. General Electric (GE) is the largest company listed on the NYSE in terms of market capitalization, which is measured by multiplying the price per share of the stock times the number of shares outstanding. Exxon Mobil and Citigroup follow GE. Shares of Berkshire-Hathaway, the company run by Warren Buffet, are the most expensive stock on the NYSE, trading for more than $70,000 each.

Trading volume on the NYSE soared in the late twentieth century. The NYSE's average trading volume now exceeds one billion shares per day, up from an average daily trading volume of 150,000 shares in 1990. This increase in trading volume could not have been accomplished without technology. Although specialists are charged with facilitating trade, approximately 85 percent of all market orders arrive on the floor of the exchange via SuperDot, an electronic trading system; more than 90 percent of these orders are executed and reported within 60 seconds. The NYSE has successfully used technology to address the challenges associated

with a dynamic, fast-paced trading environment; it boasts America's first commercial application of large-scale, flat-screen plasma technology, and the exchange is beginning to use wireless trading systems and handheld computers.

The NYSE has a distinguished history as the place where publicly traded companies raise capital. The exchange has played a prominent role in promoting free enterprise and keeping the United States at the center of world capital markets. The NYSE will remain a vital force as the trading of financial instruments continues to grow and evolve throughout the world.

Further Reading

Geisst, Charles R. *100 Years of Wall Street*. New York: McGraw-Hill, 1999.

Gitman, Lawrence J., and Michael D. Joehnk. *Fundamentals of Investing*. 8th ed. New York: Addison-Wesley, 2002.

New York Stock Exchange. *New York Stock Exchange Annual Report: 2001*. New York: New York Stock Exchange, 2001. Also available: http://www.nyse.com/annualreport/ (February 28, 2003).

———. *New York Stock Exchange Fact Book: 1999 Data*. New York: New York Stock Exchange, 2000.

Reilly, Frank K., and Edgar A. Norton. *Investments*. 5th ed. Fort Worth, Tex.: Dryden Press, 1999.

—*Angeline Lavin*

Richard Grasso, left, chairman of the New York Stock Exchange (NYSE), on the floor of the exchange with John Tate, center, CFO of Krispy Kreme Doughnuts, and Scott Livengood, right, president and CEO of Krispy Kreme. In May 2001 Krispy Kreme opened its first day of trading on the NYSE after transfering from the Nasdaq Stock Market.

Nike

The success of Nike is a classic American business tale. Phil Knight and Bill Bowerman combined their love of athletics with entrepreneurial spirit to build first an athletic shoe company, then a cultural symbol.

Knight was a shy young man who seemed to blend in with the crowd—not appearing to be the kind of man who would build a multibillion-dollar company. He participated in several sports in high school but stood out only as a successful distance runner. Upon graduation he attended college in Oregon, running track, studying business, and eventually becoming an accountant. Most people who knew him at the time agreed that he was a nice young man with a bright future, but also said that they could not remember much about him.

In contrast, Bowerman was a natural leader, having built perhaps the best track program in the country at the University of

Oregon. In 23 years his teams won four NCAA basketball championships and produced 44 All-Americans and 19 Olympians. Bowerman also had a commanding presence and was outspoken in his views. He continually lectured his athletes on how to improve their games and on the importance of strong morals. His passion for improvement touched on all aspects of track competition. He is credited with developing the concept of interval training, involving running shorter distances quickly as a way to prepare the body to run faster. He also experimented with materials for creating an all-weather track.

Bowerman believed that the canvas track shoes of the 1950s were too expensive and cumbersome. Convinced that better shoes produced better times for his athletes, he experimented with different materials to develop a superior product. Eventually he was successful and began to handcraft shoes for his team.

At about the same time, Knight had written a paper for a business class about the

Nike cofounder and CEO Phil Knight with a picture of Michael Jordan looming over his shoulder in 1999.

future of athletic shoes. In the paper Knight stated that Japanese companies had become dominant in the camera industry by learning how to produce cameras for less than the competition. He theorized that the same could happen with athletic shoes.

Shortly after he wrote his paper, Knight vacationed in Japan and found that companies there were already producing inexpensive versions of the leading Adidas track shoe. After returning to the United States, he contacted Bowerman about the new shoes, and the pair formed a partnership under the name Blue Ribbon Sports in 1962. Knight would manage the business and sell the shoes; Bowerman would test them, offer ideas for improvement, and try to convince other track coaches to use them.

Blue Ribbon shoes struggled during its first decade. Production delays, shipping problems, and quality control all posed challenges. Funds were tight and bankruptcy always seemed a possibility.

Managerial savvy and the increasing popularity of fitness in America saved the company, however. Knight foresaw a tremendous opportunity: the popularity of running was exploding at a time when the competition was both slow to innovate and too far away from the U.S. market to gauge its needs accurately. Meanwhile, in 1971 Bowerman created the modern distance-running shoe by pouring rubber into his wife's waffle iron.

Blue Ribbon successfully used two business techniques that subsequently became

Shopping for sneakers at a mall in Portland, Oregon, in 2002.

norms in the sporting goods industry. First, the company began to sponsor athletes and coaches, paying them to use company products. These athletes, including basketball, tennis, football, and track stars, wore the new Nike brand apparel, providing the company with highly visible images of success. The inclusion of college coaches in this promotional campaign increased brand recognition among the most important population of customers—young men.

Second, the company used outsourcing (contracting with other companies for performance of specific production tasks) to produce its products. Blue Ribbon concentrated on design, innovation, and image. It paid shoe companies in Asia (where wages were low) to manufacture the shoes, thus reducing its labor costs. This tactic enabled Blue Ribbon to gain a price advantage over its competitors in the United States and Europe, while increasing sales and profits. The company went public in 1980, selling shares of its stock to raise money for further expansion; at the same time Knight and Bowerman changed the corporate name to Nike (the Greek goddess of victory, associated with athletic competition and flight).

Nike hit hard times in the early 1980s when foreign competitors started using Nike's own techniques for reducing costs and increasing profits. In addition, Nike was late to recognize the potential importance of an upsurge of interest in women's aerobics. Reebok did not make this mistake and became a powerful new competitor. Nike was in serious trouble by the end of 1984.

Nike revitalized its business, however, with a series of brilliant advertising campaigns and innovative products tied to star athletes. Nike's Air Jordan commercials debuted in 1985, featuring Michael Jordan and the new Jump-Man logo. The brilliance of Jordan's athleticism combined with the appealing advertising campaign rejuvenated the company and made Jordan the most widely recognized person in the world.

Concurrently, Nike introduced the Air™ brand of cross-training shoes, which featured an air pocket for shock absorbency and could be used for a variety of sports. In a second touch of advertising brilliance, Nike also signed football and baseball star Bo Jackson to endorse the product in the "Bo knows" campaign. Again, the combination of advertising and product innovation increased sales, profits, and the status of the company; in 1991 Nike earned more than $3 billion. In the 1990s Tiger Woods—the best golfer of his time—was seen around the world sporting the Nike logo. Sales, profits, and prestige again increased while the company broadened its product line to include golf apparel and equipment.

Ironically, outsourcing—the strategy that contributed significantly to Nike's early successes—became a negative in the 1990s. Critics charged Nike with tolerating low wages and substandard working conditions in the Asian factories that produced its shoes. Others charged that Nike shoes were manufactured using materials and processes that were harmful to the

Nike

1962
Phil Knight and Bill Bowerman form Blue Ribbon Sports.

1971
Bowerman invents the modern distance-running shoe.

1980
Knight and Bowerman take company public and change name to Nike.

1985
Nike debuts Air Jordan campaign.

1991
Nike earns more than $3 billion.

In New York, members of United Students Against Sweatshops unfurl a banner accusing Nike of using sweatshop labor to produce its apparel, April 25, 2000. Nike supports the Fair Labor Association in the fight against sweatshop labor, but critics argue the association is not effective enough in ensuring safe and humane working conditions.

environment. On the strength of these criticisms, activist groups organized protests and consumer boycotts and attacked the reputation of the company. In response, Nike has attempted to gain a reputation for corporate responsibility through worker-friendly policies and an aggressive public relations campaign.

Further Reading

Katz, Donald R. *Just Do It: The Nike Spirit in the Corporate World*. Avon, Mass.: Adams Publishing, 1995.

Strasser, J. D., and Laurie Becklund. *Swoosh: The Unauthorized Story of Nike and the Men Who Played There*. New York: HarperBusiness, 1993.

—David Long

See also:
Corporation; Profit and
Loss; Taxation.

Nonprofit Entities

In the United States, a large number of different kinds of organizations are identified as worthy of tax exemption, ranging from business associations to charitable organizations and social clubs. The Salvation Army, the Republican Party, the American Heart Association, the Guggenheim Museum, and the United Automobile Workers of America are all nonprofit entities or nonprofits. Although nonprofit entities vary widely in their goals and functions, they share five critical features. To be considered part of the nonprofit sector, an entity must be an institution with some meaningful structure and permanence; not part of the apparatus of government; self-governing; non-profit-distributing (not permitted to distribute profits to its owners or directors, but rather required to reinvest them in the objectives of the organization); and supportive of some public purpose.

All organizations that meet these five criteria are formally part of the nonprofit sector in the United States; however, an important distinction exists between two broad categories of these organizations. The first category is primarily member-serving organizations. Although serving some public purpose, these organizations address the interests, needs, and desires of the members of the organization, for example, social clubs, business associations, labor unions, mutual benefit organizations of various kinds, and political parties.

The second group of nonprofit organizations is primarily devoted to public service. These organizations exist exclusively to serve the needs of a broader public audience, for example, a variety of charitable, grant-making foundations; religious congregations; and a wide range of educational, scientific, charitable, and related service organizations providing everything from nursing home care to environmental advocacy.

That nonprofit organizations play such an important role in American life is, in part, a historical accident. In most areas, American society came into existence before the government did. Frontier settlers had to find ways to provide needed public services for themselves. They did so by joining voluntarily with their neighbors to create schools and build public facilities.

America's first nonprofit corporation was Harvard College; it was founded with public subsidies in 1636. As urbanization and industrialization accelerated in the nineteenth-century United States, the limited capability of purely voluntary responses to human needs became increasingly apparent. Demand grew for government assistance and authority to address serious poverty, ill-health, inadequate housing, recurrent unemployment, and related problems. Indeed, nonprofit organizations were often in the forefront of pressing for increased government involvement.

Perhaps because of this long history, under U.S. law the formation of nonprofit organizations is considered a basic right that

Number of National Nonprofit Associations by Type 1980 to 2000			
	1980	1990	2000
Trade, business, commercial	3,118	3,918	3,880
Agriculture	677	940	1,102
Legal, governmental, public admin., military	529	792	789
Scientific, engineering, technology	1,039	1,417	1,301
Educational	12,376	1,291	1,296
Cultural	(1)	1,886	1,785
Social welfare	994	1,705	1,828
Health, medical	1,413	2,227	2,494
Public affairs	1,068	2,249	1,775
Fraternal, foreign interest, nationality, ethnic	435	573	524
Religious	797	1,172	1,122
Veteran, hereditary, patriotic	208	462	834
Hobby, avocational	910	1,475	1,329
Athletic sports	504	840	716
Labor unions	235	253	231
Chambers of Commerce[2]	105	168	142
Greek and non-Greek letter societies	318	340	295
Fan clubs	NA	581	380
Total	14,726	22,289	21,840

NA = Not available. [1]Data for cultural associations included with educational associations.
[2]National and binational.
Source: Gale Group, Farmington Hills, Mich., compiled from Encyclopedia of Associations, annual.

Every night St. John's Hospice in Philadelphia serves hundreds of meals to the homeless. Religious and charitable institutions are key parts of the nonprofit sector.

does not depend on government approval. This is particularly true of religious congregations, which are specifically exempted from obligation to register and to file the annual reporting form that registered organizations are required to submit.

Nonprofits and the Economy

The distinction between member-serving and public-serving organizations is far from perfect. Nevertheless, it is sufficiently important to find formal reflection in U.S. law. Public-serving organizations fall into a special legal category—Section 501(c)(3) of the U.S. tax code—that makes them eligible not only for exemption from federal income taxation and most state and local taxation, but also for receipt of tax-deductible gifts from individuals and corporations. Individuals and corporations can deduct the value of gifts given to these organizations from their own income in computing their tax liabilities. For its tax implications alone, this public-benefit portion of the American nonprofit sector is a major economic force.

The approximately 750,000 organizations that compose this core, public-benefit service portion of the American nonprofit sector had operating expenditures in 2000 of approximately $433 billion. If this set of organizations were a nation, its economy would thus be larger than all but 10 national economies—larger than the economies of Australia, India, Mexico, and the Netherlands. What is more, if the volunteer labor that these organizations utilize is added in, the total economic activity these organizations represent would rise by another $80 to $100 billion.

Not all portions of this nonprofit sector contribute equally to the sector's economic scale, of course. By far the largest component is the health subsector. Health organizations alone account for more than 60 percent of all nonprofit expenditures. Higher education is second with about 20 percent. The remaining 20 percent of nonprofit expenditures are split among all the other kinds of organizations—social services, arts and culture, international assistance, advocacy, community development, and many more.

Further Reading

Hutton, Stan, and Frances Phillips. *Nonprofit Kit for Dummies.* Hoboken, N.J.: John Wiley & Sons, 2001.
Riddle, John. *Streetwise Managing a Nonprofit.* Avon, Mass.: Adams Media, 2002.

—John Riddle

See also:
Balance of Payments; Balance of Trade; Globalization; International Trade; Protectionism.

North American Free Trade Agreement

The North American Free Trade Agreement (NAFTA) is an international trade accord among Canada, Mexico, and the United States that was reached in 1992, ratified in 1993, and became effective January 1, 1994. The treaty calls for a gradual elimination of all trade barriers between the three countries, creating a free flow of goods across borders unimpeded by tariffs (taxes on imports) or other forms of protectionist policies like quotas, domestic content requirements, or excessive quality standards. The final agreement was inspired by the success of the European Union and a desire on the part of Mexico to be included in the basic tenets of the 1988 Canadian and United States Trade Agreement (CUSTA; implemented January 1, 1989).

NAFTA has three important elements. First, NAFTA strives to eliminate all trade barriers among the three counties. When NAFTA was enacted, the trend in this direction was already evident. Trade barriers between the United States and Canada had been mostly removed. As Canada and Mexico had relatively little trade, the more important issue for NAFTA was the flow of goods between the United States and Mexico; a trend had begun in the mid-1980s to reduce trade barriers between the two countries. The tariffs on average for Mexican goods entering the United States, at the signing of NAFTA, were a little over 2 percent; they fell to less than 3/4 of 1 percent after the implementation of NAFTA. Mexican tariffs on U.S. goods were around 10 percent and fell to less than 3 percent. The full elimination of all trade barriers is scheduled for 2009 at the latest. All restrictive licenses, quotas, and other forms of trade protection policies will have been eliminated by then.

The second element of NAFTA stipulates that goods subject to free trade must have a specified percentage of value produced in Canada, Mexico, or the United States. This provision addresses concerns that non-NAFTA countries might take advantage of the low tariffs in one of the NAFTA countries to gain access to all three. For example, Japanese and European rivals might import components from their home countries,

On October 7, 1992, in San Antonio, Texas, the North American Free Trade Agreement was signed. Standing are President Carlos Salinas de Gortari of Mexico, left, President George H. W. Bush, center, and Prime Minister Brian Mulroney of Canada. Seated, chief trade representatives of the three countries are signing.

Preamble

The Government of Canada, the Government of the United Mexican States and the Government of the United States of America, resolved to:

Strengthen the special bonds of friendship and cooperation among their nations;

Contribute to the harmonious development and expansion of world trade and provide a catalyst to broader international cooperation;

Create an expanded and secure market for the goods and services produced in their territories;

Reduce distortions to trade;

Establish clear and mutually advantageous rules governing their trade;

Ensure a predictable commercial framework for business planning and investment;

Build on their respective rights and obligations under the General Agreement on Tariffs and Trade and other multilateral and bilateral instruments of cooperation;

Enhance the competitiveness of their firms in global markets;

Foster creativity and innovation, and promote trade in goods and services that are the subject of intellectual property rights;

Create new employment opportunities and improve working conditions and living standards in their respective territories;

Undertake each of the preceding in a manner consistent with environmental protection and conservation;

Preserve their flexibility to safeguard the public welfare;

Promote sustainable development;

Strengthen the development and enforcement of environmental laws and regulations; and

Protect, enhance and enforce basic workers' rights;

Have agreed as follows:

Article 101: Establishment of the Free Trade Area

The Parties to this Agreement, consistent with Article XXIV of the *General Agreement on Tariffs and Trade*, hereby establish a free trade area.

Article 102: Objectives

1. The objectives of this Agreement, as elaborated more specifically through its principles and rules, including national treatment, most-favored-nation treatment and transparency, are to:

   a) eliminate barriers to trade in, and facilitate the cross-border movement of, goods and services between the territories of the Parties;

   b) promote conditions of fair competition in the free trade area;

   c) increase substantially investment opportunities in the territories of the Parties;

   d) provide adequate and effective protection and enforcement of intellectual property rights in each Party's territory;

   e) create effective procedures for the implementation and application of this Agreement, for its joint administration and for the resolution of disputes; and

   f) establish a framework for further trilateral, regional and multilateral cooperation to expand and enhance the benefits of this Agreement.

2. The Parties shall interpret and apply the provisions of this Agreement in the light of its objectives set out in paragraph 1 and in accordance with applicable rules of international law.

assemble them cheaply in Mexico, and compete in the U.S. market with low-cost products. This provision, disliked by most economists as it might heighten the possibility of trade diversion, was a political compromise made to ensure the ratification of NAFTA in Canada and the United States.

Third, NAFTA has established a system of dispute resolution. Within the framework set forth in NAFTA, when a disagreement arises, a country may request an investigation. A binational panel conducts the investigation that produces a report on the matter and binds the countries to the results of their analysis. A study by Human Rights Watch found the dispute resolution system to be "underutilized" because of a lack of "political will" on the part of the member countries and the lack of an independent monitoring body. Nonetheless, this and other studies have found frequent use of the complaint mechanism, with more than 20 cases of nongovernmental organizations alleging violations of domestic labor laws in one of the member states. On a number of occasions, such complaints have helped mobilize the public to pressure corporations to desist from particular actions, for example, harassing independent union organizers. Although most complaints have been directed against Mexico, focusing in particular on organizing rights, health and safety, and forced pregnancy testing, a handful of complaints have also been filed against Canada and the United States.

Debating NAFTA

Although the treaty was negotiated by the administration of George H. W. Bush, the Clinton administration had to secure the treaty's ratification in the U.S. Congress. Ratification was by no means assured, as opposition was widespread and came from both conservative and liberal quarters.

The debate over NAFTA centered on the inclusion of the relatively less-developed Mexico with the more developed economies of the United States and Canada. U.S. industrial and agricultural interests feared stiffer competition from Mexico. Textile manufacturers and shoemakers, the trucking industry, citrus growers, and sugar producers opposed NAFTA. However, the majority of the business community supported NAFTA with the expectations of greater market access and the ability to benefit from greater economies of scale.

According to economic theory, those industries that reside in a country that has an abundance of a particular factor, for example, unskilled or low-skilled labor, will benefit and have a comparative advantage in producing and exporting those goods that are well suited to production by that factor. For Mexico, this would be true for the garment industry. In the United States, garment workers, autoworkers, and assembly line workers feared they might have their wages reduced or their jobs eliminated. In response to the concerns of organized labor in the United States, a side agreement on labor was produced, called the North American Agreement on Labor Cooperation. This agreement required both Mexico and the United States to enforce their labor laws, in particular those pertaining to minimum wages, workplace safety, and child labor. Critics of this agreement, including Human Rights Watch, have complained that enforcement of the agreement has been lax, partly because of the agreement's weak sanctions.

Environmental issues engendered another side agreement: the North American Agreement on Environmental Cooperation. This accord addresses concerns about Canadian and U.S. companies relocating to Mexico to take advantage of Mexico's less stringent enforcement of environmental statutes and regulations. The main issue was the lack of Mexican enforcement of its own environmental laws. This agreement created a mechanism to investigate environmental claims brought against

About 200 teamsters protest NAFTA trucking regulations outside the Holiday Inn in San Diego, California, in 1996.

Mexico for gaining a competitive advantage by not enforcing its environmental laws. The results of these investigations are enforced by a resolution of dispute through binding arbitration. The U.S. environmental movement split down the middle over NAFTA, with some groups, the Sierra Club for one, declaring themselves satisfied with the Environmental Cooperation agreement, and many other groups insisting that not enough is being done.

NAFTA's effect on the three economies is difficult to discern as the movement toward freer trade had already begun. However, NAFTA did provide some assurances to the business community that the trend toward openness would not be transitory. Accordingly, businesses continued to organize in expectation of long-term access to all three markets. Trade flows between the three countries have increased, particularly for Mexico.

What effect has NAFTA had on employment and labor? Employment losses and gains due to imports and exports are notoriously difficult to estimate. The U.S. government reported that 2.9 million U.S. jobs were "supported by" exports to Mexico in 2000, up from 914,000 in 1993, but remained silent on the exact number of jobs lost to imports from Mexico. Instead, the government pointed to the record-setting employment creation in the U.S. economy in the years since NAFTA went into effect, even though separating the effects of NAFTA from the general economic expansion is difficult. High levels of turnover in the U.S. labor market, however, may indicate that job creation coexisted with widespread job destruction.

At Otay Mesa, near San Diego, California, a line of trucks waits to cross the border from the United States into Mexico.

Further Reading

Carbaugh, Robert J. *International Economics.* 8th ed. Mason, Ohio: South-Western, 2002.

Gerber, James. *International Economics.* Boston: Addison-Wesley/Longman, 2001.

Krugman, Paul. "The Uncomfortable Truth about NAFTA." *Foreign Affairs* 72 (November/December 1993): 13–19.

Roberts, Russell. *The Choice: A Fable of Free Trade and Protectionism.* Upper Saddle River, N.J.: Prentice-Hall, 2001.

—*James K. Self*

See also:
Environmental Regulation;
Ergonomics; Regulation of
Business and Industry.

Occupational Safety and Health Administration

The Occupational Safety and Health Administration (OSHA) is a regulatory agency of the U.S. Department of Labor. OSHA administers the Occupational Safety and Health Act (OSH Act) of 1970, the primary federal law governing workplace safety and health. OSHA regulations cover everything from the permissible level of toxic substances in the air in buildings to ergonomic standards for offices to the size of stairway treads in factories. Because of its broad mandate, OSHA regulations cover more than 100 million employees and half a million employers, making OSHA one of the most important regulatory agencies for many businesses.

Prior to OSHA's creation, no regulatory system was in place to ensure the safety and protection of workers in the workplace. Manufacturing industries, in which threat of bodily injury was high due to the use of heavy machinery and equipment, posed great risks to their factory workers. With no means of regulated safety standards, workplace injuries occurred regularly and on a constant basis. Since OSHA's inception in 1971, workplace fatalities have been cut in half and occupational injury and illness rates have declined by 40 percent. Fatality and injury rates have continued to decline steadily, even as U.S. employment has nearly doubled, from 56 million workers at 3.5 million worksites to 105 million workers at nearly 6.9 million sites.

OSHA attempts to provide regulatory standards for all workplaces to ensure the safety and well-being of both employers and employees. For example, it has been responsible for enforcing controls on levels of asbestos and other hazardous substances in the workplace. In 2000 OSHA provided safety and health training for more than 260,000 workers and employers. In both educating employers regarding safety in the workplace and implementing legislative safety standards, OSHA hopes to ensure the right to a safe working environment for every worker.

Structure of Workplace Safety and Health Regulation

Like most government agencies, OSHA operates by issuing regulations that implement the

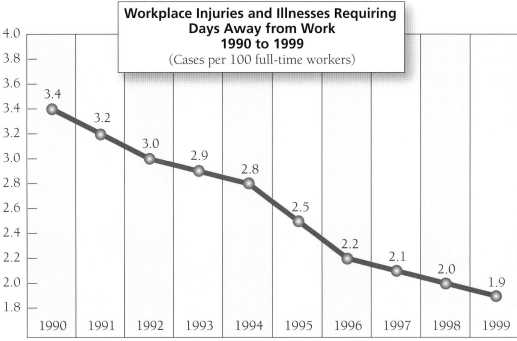

Workplace Injuries and Illnesses Requiring Days Away from Work 1990 to 1999
(Cases per 100 full-time workers)

Source: U.S. Bureau of Labor Statistics, *Incidence Rate for Cases of Workplace Injuries and Illnesses with Days Away from Work*, Private Industry, 1990–1999.

mandates of laws that were written in more general terms. OSHA has issued thousands of regulations covering virtually every aspect of workplace safety and health. The regulations are issued through a rule-making process that allows all interested groups to offer comments on OSHA's proposals. Business and labor groups also frequently seek review of OSHA regulations in the federal courts.

When Congress created the OSH Act, it split the regulation of safety and health into three parts. The National Institute for Occupational Safety and Health (NIOSH), a part of the Centers for Disease Control, conducts research into occupational health issues. OSHA uses this research in creating regulations. By separating the research and regulation-writing functions, Congress sought to ensure that research into occupational health issues is objective science and is insulated from political considerations.

The third piece of the regulatory structure is enforcement. When OSHA charges an employer with violating the OSH Act, the employer can contest the charge in a hearing before the Occupational Safety and Health Review Commission (OSHRC). The OSHRC determines whether an OSHA charge that an employer violated a regulation is correct. Both employers and OSHA can appeal decisions made by OSHRC.

OSHA shares jurisdiction over some workplace issues with other agencies. For example, the Environmental Protection Agency, the Wage and Hour Administration of the Department of Labor, and OSHA are all concerned with different aspects of field conditions for farm workers.

The OSH Act covers virtually all employers, exempting only self-employed persons, farms where only immediate family members work, and partners. Not all OSHA regulations apply to all employers, however, with many small businesses exempted from specific regulations. For example, employers with 10 or fewer employees are generally exempt from many of the OSHA record-keeping requirements.

All businesses covered by the act are subject to inspection by OSHA. If an OSHA

Occupational Safety and Health Administration

1971
Occupational Safety and Health Administration (OSHA) created.

1972
First states (South Carolina, Montana, Oregon) approved to run their own OSHA programs.

1980
Supreme Court affirms workers' rights to a safe and healthy workplace.

1992
Education Centers created to make OSHA training courses available to all employers.

2001
Congress overturns OSHA's attempt to impose ergonomic standards in the workplace.

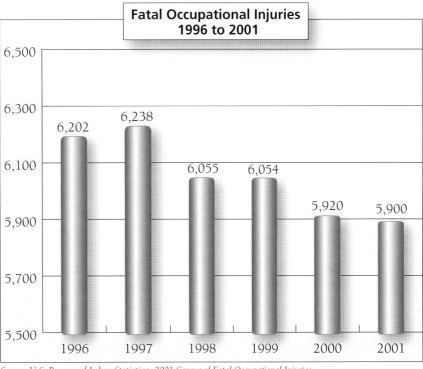

Fatal Occupational Injuries 1996 to 2001

Year	Fatalities
1996	6,202
1997	6,238
1998	6,055
1999	6,054
2000	5,920
2001	5,900

Source: U.S. Bureau of Labor Statistics, *2001 Census of Fatal Occupational Injuries,* http://www.bls.gov/iif/oshwc/cfoi/cftb0155.pdf (March 3, 2003).

inspection uncovers regulatory violations, OSHA may seek a fine or prison term, depending on the scope of the violation. OSHA regulations are numerous and complex and generally require compliance with specific standards (for example, requiring handrails on staircases or the use of respirators around a hazardous air pollutant), the keeping of records documenting compliance, and posting of information on the safety standards and employees' rights under the OSH Act.

Business Concerns about OSHA

Businesses often object to OSHA regulations on four grounds. First, they complain that OSHA does not adequately consider costs in writing regulations. For example, in 1999 OSHA published proposed standards on ergonomics regulations aimed at preventing musculo-skeletal disorders, especially those involving repetitive motion injuries like carpal tunnel syndrome. OSHA estimated that the regulations would cost $4 billion but would yield $9 billion in benefits. Business groups, however, argued that the regulations would cost many times more and would yield far fewer benefits. The standards went into effect in 2001 but were quickly overturned by Congress, largely because of concerns about cost. (In April 2002 OSHA announced a revised ergonomics program, Comprehensive Plan on Ergonomics, that attempts to address cost concerns.) An earlier attempt to force OSHA to give greater weight to costs in all regulatory actions foundered when the U.S. Supreme Court ruled that the OSH Act did not allow consideration of costs in setting health standards.

Second, businesses find many OSHA regulations overly rigid. OSHA regulations concerning air quality in the workplace, for example, often mandate the use of specific equipment. Businesses argue that they should have the freedom to determine whether controlling emissions from equipment or requiring employees to use personal

One of the more recent health threats identified by OSHA is job-related stress. In the 2002 report, Stress at Work, *the National Institute for Occupational Safety and Health prepared the following examples of stressful work conditions.*

Job Conditions That May Lead to Stress

Design of Tasks. Heavy workload, infrequent rest breaks, long work hours, and shiftwork; hectic and routine tasks that have little inherent meaning, do not utilize workers' skills, and provide little sense of control.

> *Example:* David works to the point of exhaustion. Theresa is tied to the computer, allowing little room for flexibility, self-initiative, or rest.

Management Style. Lack of participation by workers in decision making, poor communication in the organization, lack of family-friendly policies.

> *Example:* Theresa needs to get the boss's approval for everything, and the company is insensitive to her family needs.

Interpersonal Relationships. Poor social environment and lack of support or help from coworkers and supervisors.

> *Example:* Theresa's physical isolation reduces her opportunities to interact with other workers or receive help from them.

Work Roles. Conflicting or uncertain job expectations, too much responsibility, too many "hats to wear."

> *Example:* Theresa is often caught in a difficult situation trying to satisfy both customers' needs and the company's expectations.

Career Concerns. Job insecurity and lack of opportunity for growth, advancement, or promotion; rapid changes for which workers are unprepared.

> *Example:* Since the reorganization at David's plant, everyone is worried about the future of the company and what will happen next.

Environmental Conditions. Unpleasant or dangerous physical conditions such as crowding, noise, air pollution, or ergonomic problems.

> *Example:* David is exposed to constant noise at work.

Source: National Institute for Occupational Safety and Health, *Stress at Work*, 2002, http://www.cdc.gov/niosh/stresswk.html (March 3, 2003).

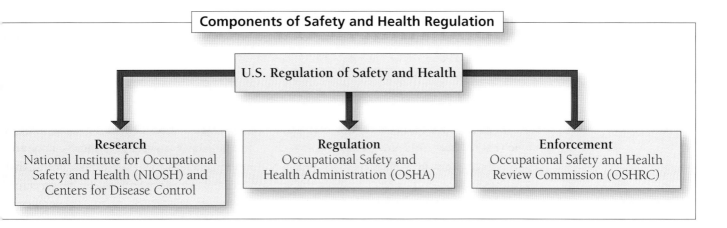

Components of Safety and Health Regulation

U.S. Regulation of Safety and Health

Research
National Institute for Occupational Safety and Health (NIOSH) and Centers for Disease Control

Regulation
Occupational Safety and Health Administration (OSHA)

Enforcement
Occupational Safety and Health Review Commission (OSHRC)

protective gear, including respirators, is the appropriate solution.

Third, businesses argue that OSHA sometimes serves as a tool of organized labor, which uses OSHA complaints against nonunion businesses to pressure nonunion employers to agree to accept unions. By instigating OSHA investigations of a nonunion plant, they argue, unions can impose significant costs, even on those employers in compliance with OSHA regulations, through productivity losses in the investigation and legal costs in preparing for OSHA inspections.

Finally, and most important, businesses are concerned that OSHA regulations are so numerous and complex that full compliance is impossible. This leaves businesses exposed to enforcement actions at any time and makes them dependent on the interpretation of regulations by any given OSHA inspector. The lack of regulatory certainty undermines the ability to predict costs and, ultimately, the rule of law.

OSHA Issues

OSHA raises important issues about the role of government in the regulation of businesses. OSHA was created to correct a perceived market failure: businesses concerned with profits would not take appropriate steps to safeguard employees' health and safety if such steps would reduce profits. This market failure analysis rested on the assumption that employees failed to perceive the risks imposed on them by employers. If employees were aware of workplace hazards, they could demand additional

compensation, eliminating the benefit to employers of not remedying the problem. Particularly with respect to hazardous substances, OSHA proponents argued that employees underestimate the risks of exposure and so fail to seek compensation for the harms suffered. OSHA, it was thought, would be able to remedy these harms.

Writing regulations to improve workplace safety and health proved to be more difficult than anticipated, however, and OSHA soon fell into political disfavor, accused by some of adopting overly rigid workplace rules that failed to improve safety or health. Ironically, OSHA has also been criticized by labor advocates for precisely the opposite—for being too promanagement in its dictates and too lax in enforcement. The controversy over OSHA's attempts to set ergonomics standards during the 2000 presidential campaign shows that OSHA regulation remains a political issue.

Further Reading

Dudley, Susan E., and Diana Rowen. *Overstressing Business: OSHA and Ergonomics.* Washington, D.C.: National Legal Center for the Public Interest, 1999.

Lofgren, Don J. *Dangerous Premises: An Insider's View of OSHA Enforcement.* Ithaca, N.Y.: ILR Press, 1989.

McGarity, Thomas O., and Sidney A. Shapiro. *Workers at Risk: The Failed Promise of the Occupational Safety and Health Administration.* Westport, Conn.: Praeger, 1993.

U.S. Senate Committee on Small Business. *Entrepreneurship in America: The Impact of OSHA and Other Agencies: Hearing before the Committee on Small Business.* 105th Cong., 1st sess., May 31, 1997.

—*Andrew Morriss*

Opportunity Cost

In thinking about cost, we ordinarily think about money: How much will a pair of new shoes or some new tires for the car cost? The concept of opportunity cost, however, refers to the cost of choices, not things, and the cost of choices is not always measured in money.

What does it mean to talk about the cost of choices? The answer is implicit in a favorite adage among economists, "There is no such thing as a free lunch." If you were to object to the adage, mentioning a time when you enjoyed a lunch that someone else paid for, an economist would reply that you could have spent your lunchtime doing something else— washing your car, perhaps, or caring for a younger sibling. In choosing to go to lunch instead, you gave up that alternative use of your time, and the value of that alternative was the real cost—the opportunity cost—of the decision to enjoy the lunch. It was not free, even though someone else paid for it.

Economists maintain that all choices entail an opportunity cost. Consider the broader context in which decisions must be made—a context marked by scarcity. We experience scarcity when we want more than we can have. Material things, including housing, food, and clothing are only the first items on our wish list. People also want education, health care, protection from criminals, clean air, good roads, mass transit systems, opportunities to travel, time to pursue hobbies, confidence in a secure retirement, and so forth. The list is endless. Society is limited, however, in what it can produce. Productive resources (labor resources, capital resources, and natural resources) are finite. As a result, choices must be made among alternative possibilities. Scarcity and choice are a universal condition applying to all societies.

For example, a teenager wakes up on Saturday morning and considers three choices:

1. Roll over and go back to sleep.

All decisions bring with them some cost: for example, choosing to go to lunch means sacrificing time that might have been spent doing something else.

2. Get up and help his parents with the grocery shopping.

3. Get up and jog two miles before breakfast.

He is looking at scarcity; he has more alternatives than time, and he will have to choose. If he decides to jog, he gives up the opportunity to sleep late. If he decides to sleep, he gives up jogging, at least for now. The opportunity cost for either choice is the value of what he did not choose.

Consider the cost of a high school education. Most young people attend public high schools; it may seem that a high school education is free because no tuition is charged. An economist would say that the real cost, the opportunity cost, of going to high school is the next-best alternative—income that might have been earned in the job market, for example, or the value of leisure time—young people give up when they choose to stay in school. A high school education is never free, even when the dollar costs are distributed among taxpayers, rather than being paid directly by students or their parents.

The analysis of opportunity cost can yield surprising insights. How much is a human life worth? It is priceless, some might say. Does this mean all people would sacrifice anything to preserve their lives? Maybe not. In many instances people risk their lives because safe, healthful living seems to come at too high a price. Many people smoke, despite the advice of the surgeon general. Some play football or climb mountains or drive too fast, despite the risk of accident and injury. Some work at jobs that put them at risk of death. They choose the satisfaction they derive from risky behavior over safer or healthier options (choosing to be a nonsmoker, for example, or choosing to be an accountant rather than a firefighter). Sometimes these choices seem foolish, sometimes they seem heroic; either way, the concept of opportunity cost enables us to describe and explain these choices.

Opportunity cost is fundamental to business decisions. Business leaders constantly seek to measure opportunity costs and keep them as low as possible. Consider a grocery

Sometimes people choose risky activities—football, for example—because they accept the risk of injury as a cost of the activity.

store with 25 rows of shelving for displaying groceries. What is the opportunity cost of offering one brand of potato chips or coffee over another? What is the opportunity cost of removing a shelf to make space for a new advertising display? If the owner borrows money to expand her parking lot, will she have to drop plans for adding a floral department? In each instance of choice, which opportunity cost can the business best afford to pay? Such decisions, taken together, are critical to business success.

Further Reading

Friedman, Milton. *There's No Such Thing as a Free Lunch.* LaSalle, Ill.: Open Count Publishing, 1975.
Heyne, Paul. *The Economic Way of Thinking.* New York: Macmillan College Publishing, 1994.

—*Mark C. Schug*

See also:

Globalization; World Bank;
World Trade Organization.

Organization for Economic Cooperation and Development

The Organization for Economic Cooperation and Development (OECD) is an international organization of nations formed in 1961 to pursue global economic growth and stability. The organization is a forum for members to discuss, develop, and refine social and economic policies. The OECD is one of the most important international organizations in the world, with an annual budget greater than $200 million. The 30 member countries of this Paris-based organization produce about 60 percent of the world's goods and services. Some critics charge that the OECD is primarily designed to benefit wealthy nations, and that its decisions reflect the agendas chiefly of the European Union, Japan, and the United States.

The origins of the OECD date to 1947. In that year, European and North American nations formed the Organization for European Economic Cooperation to administer American and Canadian aid for the reconstruction of postwar Europe under the Marshall Plan.

The OECD is one of the world's largest and most reliable sources of comparable statistical, economic, and social data. Exchanges between member states flow from information and analysis provided by the Secretariat. Various departments of the Secretariat collect data, monitor trends, analyze, and forecast developments, while others research social changes or evolving patterns in trade, environment, agriculture, technology, and taxation.

Member countries compare experiences, seek answers to common problems, and work to coordinate domestic and international policies to help members and nonmembers function and prosper in an increasingly globalized world. Their exchanges may lead to agreements to act in a formal way—for example, by establishing legally

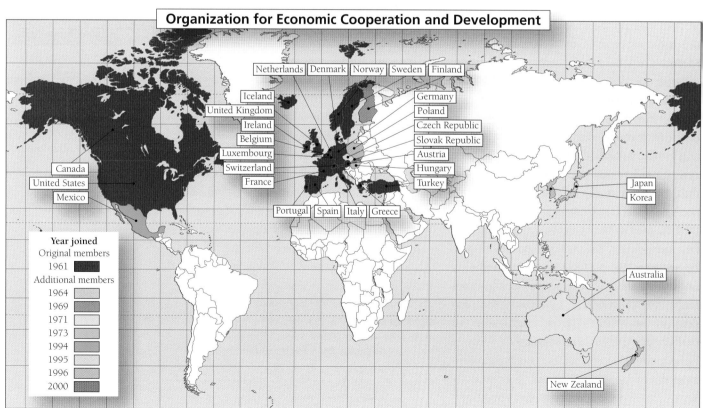

Source: Organization for Economic Cooperation and Development, www.oecd.org (March 12, 2003).

binding agreements to prohibit bribery or codes to assure the free flow of capital across borders. The OECD is also known for "soft law"—nonbinding instruments on difficult issues like guidelines for multinational enterprises. Beyond agreements, the discussions at the OECD make for better-informed work within member countries' own governments in public policy and help clarify the effect of national policies on the international community.

Member countries meet and exchange information in committees. They assemble representatives from member countries, either from national administrations or permanent delegations to the OECD in Paris. The most powerful decision-making body is the Council, which is composed of one representative from each member nation and a representative from the European Union. The Council meets regularly at the OECD ambassador level and once per year at the ministerial level. Due to the perception that the OECD is a tool of wealthy nations, these meetings sometimes inspire anti-globalization protests similar to those sometimes seen at meetings of the World Trade Organization.

Specialized committees (of which there are approximately 200) meet to advance ideas and review progress in defined areas of policy, including, trade, money laundering by international terrorists, food safety, poverty, electronic commerce, science and technology, development assistance, and financial markets. Approximately 40,000 senior officials from national administrations attend OECD committee meetings each year to inquire, review, and contribute to work undertaken by the Secretariat.

The OECD has two official languages: English and French. Staff members are citizens of OECD countries but serve as international civil servants with no national affiliation during their posting. The OECD is funded by member nations. Contributions to the OECD annual budget are based on a formula tied to the size of a nation's economy. The United States provides 25 percent of the OECD budget; Japan is the second largest contributor.

Police and protesters clash during an anti-OECD demonstration in Bologna, Italy, in June 2000.

The emergence of globalization has seen the scope of the OECD's work move from examination of each policy area within member states to analysis of how various policy areas interact between OECD countries and beyond OECD areas. The OECD has a cooperative relationship with about 70 nations, and nonmembers have increasingly been invited to subscribe to OECD agreements. In such areas as eliminating harmful tax practices and combating terrorist and other illicit use of global financial systems, the OECD is working with nonmember economies to find solutions acceptable to all. The Centre for Cooperation with Non-Members (CCNM), established in 1998, is the focal point for these relationships. It manages multicountry programs linked to core themes—for example, trade and the environment—of OECD work, as well as individual country programs with major nonmember economies including Brazil, China, and Russia.

Further Reading

Henry, Miriam. *The OECD, Globalization, and Education Policy.* New York: Pergamon, 2001.
Organization for Economic Cooperation and Development. *Open Markets Matter: The Benefits of Trade and Investment Liberalization.* Paris: Organization for Economic Cooperation and Development, 1998.

—*Carl Pacini*

See also:
Energy Industry;
Environmentalism; Price
Fixing; Supply and Demand.

Organization of Petroleum Exporting Countries

The Organization of Petroleum Exporting Countries (OPEC) is an association of 11 developing nations with revenues heavily dependent on the production and export of oil. OPEC, commonly referred to as a cartel, coordinates its members' crude oil production policies in an attempt to maintain stable world oil prices and a steady supply of oil to consuming countries. Since the 1960s OPEC has been a major influence on the world market for oil.

Representatives from five nations—Iran, Iraq, Kuwait, Saudi Arabia, and Venezuela—founded OPEC on September 14, 1960, at a meeting in Baghdad, Iraq. In

the late 1950s the petroleum industries of these countries were controlled by U.S. and Western European oil companies, who extracted crude oil and sold it on the world market at posted prices—prices kept artificially low by the oil companies. The host governments then received payments, known as royalties, based on the revenues of these companies. Production quantities varied widely from one year to the next, as the oil firms operated independently of one another.

In 1959 and 1960 oil production outpaced demand, prompting several of the oil companies to reduce their posted prices, thus reducing their profits and the royalties paid to the host governments. OPEC was formed in response to this unexpected drop in national income. In addition to forming the cartel, some of the countries also nationalized the oil producing and refining equipment of the petroleum companies through buying out the Western firms or negotiating better terms,

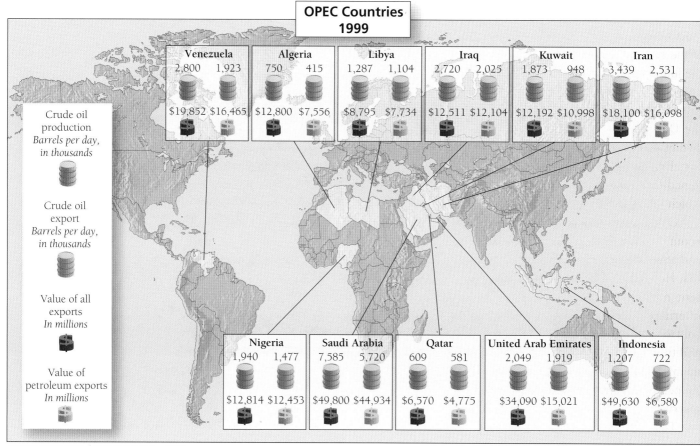

Source: OPEC Annual Statistical Bulletin, 1999.

OPEC leaders during a summit in 2000: (left to right) the emir of Qatar, Sheik Hamad ben Khalifa ben Hamed Al Thani; Iraqi vice president Taha Yassin Ramadan; Iranian president Seyyed Mohammad Khatami; Libyan colonel Mustafa Al-Kharroubi; and Algerian president Abdelaziz Bouteflika.

which gave greater pricing control to the local governments.

Membership in OPEC, according to the organization's charter, is open to any country with substantial exports of crude oil and interests similar to those of the member countries. Any application for membership must be approved by at least three-quarters of the current members, including all five of the founding members. Current members of OPEC are: Algeria, Indonesia, Iran, Iraq, Kuwait, Libya, Nigeria, Qatar, Saudi Arabia, the United Arab Emirates, and Venezuela. Two other countries have participated in the cartel since its founding: Ecuador, which joined in 1973 and left in 1992, and Gabon, which joined in 1975 and left in 1994.

OPEC members collectively produce about 41 percent of the world's crude oil and about 15 percent of the world's natural gas. However, OPEC's exports of oil represent nearly 55 percent of the oil traded internationally. Although OPEC does not control the oil market, the cartel has the ability to significantly affect it—in 2001 its members collectively possessed more than 77 percent of the world's known crude oil reserves.

The supreme authority of OPEC is its conference, which consists of delegations from member countries and which meets at least twice a year—in March and September—and in extra sessions if necessary. At the conference, members analyze and discuss the current conditions in the world oil markets and make forecasts; they also make decisions about OPEC's future oil production policies. All decisions must be approved unanimously, and each country gets one vote in all matters.

OPEC's main tool for affecting the oil market is the setting of production ceilings for each member nation. These ceilings limit the amount of oil that the country can produce in a given time. Although formally every member retains absolute power of final decision about its production policies, once the ceilings are allocated at a conference and all delegations unanimously agree to the allocation, the countries must comply with the organization's decision.

OPEC has had mixed success in achieving its goals of oil price stabilization and support for steady demand. In the 1960s production expanded as demand grew at a very fast rate, so the cartel had little control over the supply of oil. However, by the 1970s the demand began to outgrow the supply of oil in non-OPEC countries. In 1973 OPEC raised its oil prices, triggering

Organization of Petroleum Exporting Countries   969

A gas station in Connecticut during the mid-1970s oil crisis.

what eventually became known as the first oil crisis. The effect of higher oil prices was exacerbated by the Arab–Israeli war of 1973, during which the Arab members of OPEC stopped their exports of oil to countries supporting Israel. As a result, oil prices in the United States and the countries of Western Europe rose sharply and supplies became scarce.

During the 1980s OPEC set production ceilings for its members several times. However, several cartel nations ignored their limits. Consequently, supply of oil exceeded demand, and in 1983 OPEC was forced to cut its prices for the first time.

In the early 1990s oil prices remained relatively stable, with the notable exception of a brief price increase following Iraq's invasion of Kuwait in 1990. In the late twentieth century OPEC's influence on the oil market was limited by the actions of

other oil-producing countries, notably Russia. Russian oil companies pursue their own goals, which often involve expanding output; this, in turn, undermines the effect of any output contraction by the cartel. Not until the 1990s were Russian oil exports significant enough to affect OPEC's control of oil markets. As the cartel does not have perfect control of the world's supply of oil, its future success will depend on its ability to coordinate its actions with those of other oil-rich nations.

Further Reading

Ghanem, Shukri Mohammed. *OPEC: The Rise and Fall of an Exclusive Club.* London and New York: KPI, 1986.

Kohl, Wilfrid L., ed. *After the Oil Price Collapse: OPEC, the United States, and the World Oil Market.* Baltimore, Md.: Johns Hopkins University Press, 1991.

—*Mikhail Kouliavtsev*

Outsourcing

Outsourcing is the practice of obtaining a product or services from external providers. Parents outsource child care when they drop their children off at the day care center; office managers outsource maintenance when they contract for custodial services. The parents could stay home and take care of the children themselves, of course, and the office manager could mop the floors and empty the wastebaskets at night. By obtaining these services from others, however, the clients in each case expect to realize a number of benefits because the outsourcing arrangement enables them to focus on their core competencies—to spend more time doing what they do best. The benefits of outsourcing typically include improved efficiency and quality as well as reduced costs.

Widespread use of outsourcing is recent in the business world. Not long ago, the strategy in many industries was for businesses to seek economy and efficiency by consolidating many operations under one corporate roof. Late in the nineteenth

See also:
Comparative Advantage;
Economies of Scale;
Edison Schools, Inc.

Vertical integration involves the consolidation of as many business operations as possible; outsourcing, on the other hand, involves a collection of relationships with subcontractors.

Vertical Integration vs. Outsourcing

Vertical Integration Model

Yesteryear Steel Corp. =

Mining fields

+

Manufacturing facilities

+

Distribution facilities

Outsourcing Model

Contemporary Steel Corp. =

Raw Materials Inc. ⟷

Contemporary Steel Corp. ⟷

Fastrack Shipping Co.

century, for example, John D. Rockefeller founded and managed the Standard Oil Company through an approach now known as vertical integration. Vertical integration allowed Standard Oil to own and operate not only its oil wells and refineries but also the storage facilities, railroad tank cars, barrel-making factories, and other units responsible for the production, marketing, and distribution of its products.

By the mid-twentieth century such corporate structuring was growing obsolete. Competitive pressures and consumer demand increasingly pushed suppliers of goods and services to control costs while offering special products and services and improved quality. Outsourcing helped many businesses to respond to these pressures, especially in their handling of administrative services, computer network support, and payroll operations. Even in the age of the Internet, for example, law firms and insurance companies still operate mail rooms to handle large volumes of incoming and outgoing U.S. mail. These firms could maintain their own staffs to operate their mailrooms, but the management and maintenance of mail services would divert resources from the practice of law or the writing, selling, and servicing of insurance policies. A lawyer whose specialty is mergers and acquisitions, for example, might need to spend some time every week supervising the mailroom staff, or supervising the mailroom supervisor. The firm would rather see that lawyer spend her time on her core competency—

Benefits of Outsourcing

- Cost reduction
- Personnel reduction
- Capital investment relief
- Better technology
- Improved quality
- Flexibility in delivery of service
- Extra management time

Source: Charles L. Gay, *Inside Outsourcing: An Insider's Guide to Managing Strategic Sourcing*, London, Nicholas Brealey Publishing, 2000.

handling mergers and acquisitions, not mail. As a result, the firm might contract with an outsourcing business to provide mailroom resources: labor, equipment, and industry expertise.

A successful relationship between a client firm and an outsourcing provider depends on two critical understandings. One has to do with costs; the other, with the client firm's ability to control its own products and services.

At first glance, the products or services provided by an outsourcing organization may seem costly, but appropriately designed outsourcing arrangements produce savings for many clients in the long run. Outsourcing organizations focus on providing a given product or service. By providing that product or service to law firms, insurance firms, and other companies having similar needs, outsourcing firms can achieve economies of scale that individual firms—even large, multinational firms—could never achieve. In focusing on mailroom services, for example, an outsourcing firm dedicates its resources to recruiting, hiring, and training mailroom workers, and to research and development in process engineering, equipment procurement, cost containment, and quality management. Client firms from any number of industries dependent on mailroom services benefit from the expertise and economies of scale produced by such specialization.

Outsourcing might seem to imply that a client firm would lose a measure of control over its operations. If somebody else is handling the payroll or delivery service, perhaps the client firm's own quality standards will not be met. In fact, however, a client firm can strengthen its control over key operations through contractual expectations for production, delivery, and application of a product or service consistent with its own business cycles.

Contractual arrangements geared to business cycles might result in a client firm not investing in labor or equipment needed only for a special, short-term project. Landscaping firms, for example, require different staffing levels at different times of the

year, with peak demand often occurring in the spring. Outsourcing for additional, short-term labor from a temporary agency is one option for landscaping firms at such times. Temporary services are typically responsible for all costs associated with their employees. In contracting for temporary services, therefore, a client firm can avoid the costs that would be incurred in hiring workers for a short time and then releasing them when demand falls. Providing labor and specialty equipment is of interest to an outsourcing firm because other clients may need those same resources at different times of the year. The easy, flexible application of an outsourcing firm's resources can add significant value to the client–outsourcer relationship.

Not everyone likes outsourcing. Workers in traditionally integrated firms—for example the automobile industry—have objected to cost-cutting plans calling for the outsourcing of specific production or assembly tasks. Teachers' unions, similarly, have resisted some states' new legal provisions permitting school districts to contract with outsourcers for administrative and instructional services. In these disputes, each side claims to have consumers' interests in mind. Management

claims that lower production costs and flexibility will translate into lower prices and better quality for consumers; organized workers claim that quality standards will yield to expedience in a corporate search for profits.

Although disputes of this kind will continue to arise, with resolutions influenced by political activity as well as market forces, outsourcing seems to be established in the economy. It offers the potential for mutually beneficial transactions between clients and outsourcing providers. Many modern manufacturing and service firms find that outsourcing permits them to respond more effectively and efficiently to market demands.

Further Reading

Bendor-Samuel, Peter. *Turning Lead into Gold: The Demystification of Outsourcing.* Provo, Utah: Executive Excellence Publishing, 2000.

Gay, Charles L. *Inside Outsourcing: An Insider's Guide to Managing Strategic Sourcing.* London: Nicholas Brealey Publishing, 2000.

Johnson, Mike. *Outsourcing...In Brief.* Woburn, Mass.: Butterworth-Heinemann, 1997.

Rothery, Brian, and Ian Robertson. *The Truth about Outsourcing.* Brookfield, Vt.: Gower, 1995.

—*John Western*

Large firms frequently outsource their mailroom operations.

Overhead

Overhead is the expenses or costs required to run a business that cannot be directly linked to the process of producing a product or service. Companies must allocate overhead costs to each business process to understand the profitability of each business line. Difficulties arise because each business uses overhead resources differently, and management must determine a reasonable allocation methodology.

Direct vs. Overhead Costs

A company's expenses can be broken into two categories: direct costs and indirect costs (another name for overhead). Direct costs are costs to the business that can be precisely traced to a product or service. Direct costs can be separated into direct materials and direct labor. If a company produces both automobiles and chairs, producing each automobile and chair will involve both direct materials and direct labor costs. Direct materials used to produce each automobile are the engine, the tires, the seats, and so on. The cost applied to each automobile is the actual cost to the company to buy each piece of material (for example, $5,000 for the engine, $425 for the tires, and $690 for the seats).

Direct labor is the hours employees spend working on each automobile times their hourly wage. For example, if the engine assembler is paid $15 per hour and five hours are needed to assemble the engine, the direct labor for the engine is $75. The direct material costs to produce the chair are the wood, the cushion, and nails. The direct labor costs are the hours people spend producing each chair times their hourly wage.

Next, consider all of the indirect costs to produce goods or services. Overhead encompasses three categories: manufacturing overhead, indirect labor, and nonmanufacturing overhead. Manufacturing overhead can be defined as all costs of manufacturing the product excluding direct materials and direct labor. In the example of automobiles and chairs, the factory facility that houses all of the conveyer belts and line workers, the factory's light and heat, insurance, the cost of any machines used in production, and the cost to maintain and repair the machines are considered manufacturing overhead costs. Indirect labor includes the labor costs of those who work for the company but do not directly assemble products, for example, janitors, supervisors, materials handlers, engineers, and security guards.

Finally, nonmanufacturing costs generally include marketing and selling costs and administrative costs. Marketing and selling costs include the expenditures necessary to secure customer orders and get the finished product or service delivered to the customer. These costs include advertising and shipping. Administrative costs include all executive, organizational, and clerical costs that are not included under production or marketing, for example, accounting, executive salaries and bonuses, and public relations.

The examples above identify costs associated with tangible goods. The same issues arise with service companies, which have very few direct and indirect material costs but many more direct and indirect labor costs.

Allocation of Overhead

Managers at every company must determine the profitability of a product or service line. In our example above, the company sells two products. Each product has a selling price (assume a car sells for $20,000 and a chair sells for $50); each product also has direct material and labor costs associated with its production (assume a car has $7,500 direct costs and a chair has $15). However, the profit on a car is

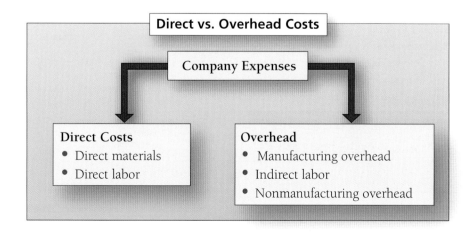

Direct vs. Overhead Costs

Company Expenses

Direct Costs
- Direct materials
- Direct labor

Overhead
- Manufacturing overhead
- Indirect labor
- Nonmanufacturing overhead

not simply $12,500 ($20,000 − $7,500). Significant investments were made to generate this profit and significant ongoing work is performed to maintain that profitability.

Therefore, to understand the profitability of the automobile and the chair, the company must allocate overhead costs to each product. To do so, an appropriate allocation base must be chosen for each overhead cost. For example, the light and heat in the factory cost $10,000 per year and are used when each production line is running. Therefore, the cost should be allocated based on the number of hours each line is operating. Assume that the automobile production line runs for 1,950 hours per year and the chair line runs 875 hours per year. The allocation percentage is calculated as follows:

For automobiles: 1,950 / (1,950 + 875) = 69% of the total cost
For chairs: 875 / (1,950 + 875) = 31% of the total cost

Thus, $6,900 ($10,000 × .69) should be deducted from the annual automobile profits and $3,100 ($10,000 × .31) should be deducted from the annual chair profits for the use of electricity and heat in the factory. These calculations are repeated for all other overhead costs until they are all allocated to either automobiles or chairs. It is important to remember to choose the correct allocation base for each cost. Some of the allocation bases for the overhead costs are:

- Cost of factory rental—square footage used by each product
- Insurance—cost of inventory held in the factory for each product
- Executive salaries—time spent on each product

As corporations invest more and more money in research and development for the creation of robots and machines to run assembly lines, overhead expenses will increase and companies will have to assure correct allocation of overhead. To understand the true profitability of each product, understanding how corporations allocate costs is imperative.

The salaries of these workers, the rent (or mortgage) on the factory, and the electricity required to run the machines all constitute overhead expenses to this salmon cannery.

Further Reading
Fremgen, James. *Allocation of Corporate Indirect Costs*. Montvale, N.J.: Institute of Management Accountants, 1981.
Innes, John, and Falconer Mitchell. *Overhead Cost*. Independence, Ky.: Thomson Learning, 1993.
Kaplan, Robert S., and Robin Cooper. *Cost and Effect: Using Integrated Cost Systems to Drive Profitability and Performance*. Boston: Harvard Business School Press, 1997.

—David Korb and Andréa Korb

Elements of Overhead for a Manufacturing Company

Manufacturing overhead
- Factory facility
- Utilities
- Insurance
- Cost of machines
- Cost of maintenance and repair of machines

Marketing and selling costs
- Advertising
- Marketing
- Shipping

Indirect labor costs
- Supervisors
- Janitors
- Materials handlers
- Engineers
- Security guards

Administrative costs
- Accounting
- Executive salaries and bonuses
- Public relations

See also:
Corporation; Investment;
Liability; Small Business.

Partnership

A partnership comes into being when two or more people join together to run a business venture and share in the profits of that venture. Partnerships are one of the oldest business forms known: references to business partnerships are found in 4,000-year-old Babylonian legal codes. Indeed, partner and partnership have meanings that extend far beyond the business world, even being used to describe long-term romantic relationships.

Although specific laws apply to business partnerships, a partnership is a far less formal business entity than is a corporation. In legal terms, a corporation is an independent entity not unlike a person. In contrast, a partnership is a legally recognized relationship between people, much like a marriage—partnerships are often called "business marriages." People involved in a business partnership share assets and liabilities and are expected to behave in a certain way toward their partners. Exiting a

partnership can be no less difficult than obtaining a divorce.

Partnerships are a popular business form for small businesses, as well as some large ones—law and accounting firms are usually partnerships, even if they are quite sizable. Forming a partnership is easy—indeed the relative lack of paperwork involved is a major reason for entering into partnerships rather than forming corporations. In the United States, most states, which govern partnerships, base their laws on the Uniform Partnership Act; accordingly, laws vary little from state to state.

Creating a Partnership

No license is required to start a partnership. Indeed, no written agreement is required—a verbal or handshake agreement is sufficient. Most states do not require a written agreement to start a partnership; however, other aspects of state business law—for instance, antifraud statutes—may serve to encourage partners to draw up a written agreement.

Written partnership agreements have other benefits. They serve as a record of the initial agreement, which can prove useful if a conflict arises between partners. If partners do not specify terms in a written agreement and terms of a verbal agreement cannot be determined, then various provisions of state law will dictate the terms of the partnership.

A partnership agreement usually specifies what the partners bring to the business venture and what they can expect to take away. For example, two people might join in a business partnership to open a dog grooming shop. One partner might contribute $30,000 to the business, the other $20,000. In exchange, the first partner has a 60 percent ownership stake in the business and receives 60 percent of any profits, while the other gets 40 percent.

Partnership agreements can be open-ended, as in the case of the dog grooming shop, or they can be designed to last only a short while, a situation called a joint venture. For example, drilling oil wells is extremely expensive, so several small oil

Partnerships: By Industry 1998 (in thousands)	Number of partnerships	Number of partners
Agriculture, forestry, fishing, and hunting	116	535
Mining	29	1,063
Utilities	2	50
Construction	126	422
Manufacturing	35	225
Wholesale trade	26	102
Retail trade	104	310
Transportation and warehousing	19	308
Information	22	359
Finance and insurance	209	3,374
Real estate	812	7,207
Professional, scientific, and technical services	118	478
Educational services	5	12
Health care and social assistance	38	205
Arts, entertainment, and recreation	30	218
Accommodation and food services	58	296
Total	1,855	15,663

Note: Covers active partnerships only. All figures are estimates based on samples.
Source: U.S. Internal Revenue Service, *Statistics of Income*, various issues.

companies will form a joint venture to drill a particular field for a limited time.

While prospective partners often bring cash to the partnership, they may provide other assets as well. Indeed, partners rarely bring only cash—those who bring nothing but cash are called silent partners. Traditional partners, in contrast, usually expect to play major roles in running the business, roles that can be specified in the agreement. One partner might agree to do a particular job—keep the books or groom the dogs, for example. Especially when more than two people are involved, one partner usually agrees to be the managing partner, or the person in charge of day-to-day operations of the business.

A partner might bring in some property of value. As with cash, that property becomes the property of the partnership, not the partner. Say four people get together to start a partnership landscaping yards. Three of them contribute cash or labor, but the fourth contributes a $12,000 truck. That truck is no longer his—instead, he now owns a quarter-share of the truck's value. If the fourth man decides to reclaim his truck and takes it back without reaching some agreement with his partners, he is appropriating the partnership's property for his personal use.

Partnerships and Liability

A participant in a partnership can lose a lot more than a truck. Unlike investors in corporations, who can lose only the amount of money they have invested, participants in a partnership are exposed to unlimited liability:

Different partners might bring different strengths to a business partnership: one partner might have more cash, for example, while another might possess greater expertise.

if the business owes someone money, the creditor can come after the personal property of the partners to get restitution.

For example, the landscapers are cutting down a tree in a client's yard, and the tree falls on the client's house. The client sues to recover the cost of repairing the damage to the house and wins a large damage award. However, the landscape business is so new, it has no money. Assuming the business has no insurance against this kind of exposure to liability, the angry client can pursue the partners' private assets—including savings accounts, homes, and vehicles—to get money.

Partners in a partnership are also exposed to joint and several liability. For example, perhaps three of the landscaping partners are poor—they put all they had into that business—and one of them is wealthy. The wealthy partner can be forced to pay the entire cost of the judgment, not just one-quarter of the amount. Thus, as in a marriage, the people involved in a business partnership would be wise to get to know each other well before agreeing to enter into a partnership. If one partner spends money foolishly, or steals from customers, or cannot fell a tree in the right direction, the other partners can be liable for whatever costs that one partner incurs for the business.

Because the consequences of one partner's misbehavior can be dire for the others, partners are legally required to act in the best business interests of the partnership. A partner cannot conceal promising business opportunities from the partnership, for example. Partners cannot work for competing businesses. Partners who fail to act in the interests of the partnership can be sued by the remaining partners.

Usually a partner gets a share of the business's profits and an ownership stake. A partnership can retain some of its business profits to fund future growth, but a substantial portion of the profits must be paid out to the partners every year. Unlike a corporation, a partnership pays no taxes. Instead, the partners pay taxes on the money paid to them by the partnership. A partner may, in addition, get a salary from the partnership.

If a partner leaves a partnership, then technically that partnership dissolves. If the exit is planned and occurs in an orderly fashion, then the remaining partners can quickly draw up a new partnership agreement so the underlying business is unaffected. The same occurs if a new partner joins the partnership. If all the partners cannot agree on whether a new person should be accepted as a partner, or if they disagree about how to treat a partner who wants to exit, the situation can deteriorate. Usually the partner who wants to leave needs to dispose of his share in the business, and disagreements sometimes occur over how

Partnerships: Selected Income and Balance Sheet Items 1980 to 1998 (in billions of dollars)						
	1980	1990	1992	1994	1996	1998
Assets	598	1,735	1,907	2,295	3,368	5,127
Liabilities	489	1,415	1,508	1,662	2,235	3,151
Receipts	292	566	597	762	1,089	1,603
Cost of goods sold/operations	114	243	249	335	486	737
Salaries and wages	22	56	62	70	94	143
Depreciation	22	60	60	22	29	43
Net income (less loss)	8	17	43	82	145	187
Net income	45	116	122	151	228	298

Note: Covers active partnerships only. All figures are estimates based on samples.
Source: U.S. Internal Revenue Service, *Statistics of Income,* various issues.

Advantages and Disadvantages of Partnerships

	Advantages	Disadvantages
General partnerships	• Permits more than one owner • Easy to form and operate • Flexible enough to adapt to changing needs	• Unlimited liability • Dissolves on death or withdrawal of partner unless safeguards are in place
Limited partnerships	• Limited liability • No limit on number of members, who can be individuals, trusts, or corporations • Greater management choice: member can manage partnership or hire professional manager	• Transfer of interest may be restricted • Costs more to form and maintain than general partnership

much that share is worth and how it should be distributed. A partner can transfer his interest in a partnership to someone the other partners do not accept, but in that case the new person's rights as a partner are extremely limited.

Limited Partnerships

If a partnership wants to raise money from outsiders, but the partners do not want to add a new partner, then the partners can offer something called a limited partnership. A limited partnership is essentially a contract between an investor and a business that specifies how much money the investor will put into the business, and what kind of returns the investor can expect.

Buying into a limited partnership is very different from forming an ordinary, or general, partnership, and much more like buying shares of a corporation. A limited partner is by definition an outsider risking money on someone else's business, so limited partnerships are far more heavily regulated than are general partnerships. In addition, the different kinds of partners have greatly differing roles. A general partner usually helps run the business; a limited partner is strongly discouraged from doing so. A general partner has to work in the best interests of the partnership; a limited partner operates under no such restriction.

If a limited partner begins to act like a general partner—becoming involved in the operations of a business, for example—then the law begins to treat her like a general partner. The most significant change is in the limited partner's liability. As a limited partner is essentially an investor, she has limited liability, which means she can lose only as much money on a business as she invested in it. However, if a limited partner starts taking an active role in the business, she can take on the unlimited liability of a general partner.

For all the risks involved with partnerships, most work out relatively well. Partnerships allow businesspeople to easily pool skills and resources to a degree that is generally not possible for a business owned by a single proprietor. Indeed, partnerships will probably remain a popular business form for the next 4,000 years.

Further Reading
Bean, Gerard M. D. *Fiduciary Obligations and Joint Ventures: The Collaborative Fiduciary Relationship.* Oxford: Clarendon Press, 1995.
Clifford, Dennis, and Ralph Warner. *The Partnership Book: How to Write a Partnership Agreement.* 6th ed. Berkeley, Calif.: Nolo Press, 2001.
Davidson, Robert L., III. *The Small Business Partnership Kit.* New York: John Wiley & Sons, 1993.
Genefke, Jens, and Frank McDonald, eds. *Effective Collaboration: Managing the Obstacles to Success.* New York: Palgrave, 2001.

—*Mary Sisson*

Patent

A patent is a legal instrument granting an inventor exclusive rights to use and benefit from his or her invention for a definite period of time. Patents are granted to encourage inventors to do their creative work.

Patents find their roots in Greek society. In his *Politics*, Aristotle referred to patents in discussing the need for a reward system for inventors. The city-state of Venice adopted the first patent law in the late 1400s. In the seventeenth century the British enacted a law that allowed for a review of all patents so that those not based on true inventions could be eliminated. Patents were introduced in the American colonies between 1640 and 1776 and were awarded at that time by individual colonies.

Modern patent law in the United States derives from the U.S. Constitution, adopted in 1789. To maintain uniformity in the granting of patents, the U.S. Constitution provides that Congress shall have the power to "promote the Progress of Science and useful Arts, by securing for limited Times to Authors and Inventors the exclusive right to their respective Writings and Discoveries." Congress passed the first Patent Act in 1790. Thomas Jefferson was an early administrator of the patent system and the author of the Patent Act of 1793. Current patent law is based on the 1952 Patent Act and its 1995 amendments.

A patent establishes the inventor's ownership of his or her invention. Ownership allows the inventor to exclude others from making, using, selling, or importing the invention for a definite term (length of time). In the United States, the term of a patent is 20 years (14 years for a design).

Under U.S. patent law, some inventions (a device that might threaten national security, for example) cannot be patented. Nor can patents be obtained on principles or laws of nature, on naturally occurring items, or inventions requiring only mental activity or processes. (Copyrights and trademarks protect inventions derived from mental processes.) The patents that may be issued in the United States are utility patents, design patents, and plant patents.

Utility Patents

Five classes of inventions may be the subject of a utility patent. One class is processes or methods—steps performed on a material, composition, or object, changing its nature or characteristics to produce a useful commodity. Examples include a process for making a chemical compound—paint, for instance—or for treating wool or linen.

Another class is machines—mechanical devices (with moving parts) that accomplish a task. Examples include a dishwasher, carburetor, lawn mower, or washing machine.

A third class is articles of manufacture—articles produced from raw or prepared materials that take on new forms, qualities, or properties. Such articles have no moving parts. Examples include a toothbrush, a table, a bench, or a golf ball.

Web Resources on Patents

patents.cos.com is a comprehensive database for all U.S. patents issued since 1975.

www.uspto.gov is the home page for the United States Patent and Trademark Office.

www.nolo.com/lawcenter provides general information and resources on various legal concepts, including patents.

www.ipwatchdog.com/patent.html provides information and resource links for patent law.

www.micropat.com/0/index9809.html is a leading Web resource of searchable collections of patent and trademark information.

www.law.cornell.edu/topics/patent.html, a site maintained by the Legal Information Institute, offers information and resources on patent law.

www.bustpatents.com provides legal tools and information on Internet patents.

www.patentcafe.com offers a patent search, plus patent, trademark, and intellectual property information for inventors, attorneys, and entrepreneurs.

www.patentgopher.com is an inexpensive patent-retrieval service that delivers patents via e-mail or direct download.

www.younginventors.com is the home page of a nonprofit organization providing young inventors and innovators with support and information.

patents1.ic.gc.ca is the home page for the Canadian Intellectual Property Office and the Canadian patents database.

A fourth class is composition of matter. The composition may be a chemical compound or a mixture of ingredients. Examples include formulations for toothpaste, shampoo, cleaning solution, or glue. The fifth class is any improvement to an invention from any of the first four classes.

Two new kinds of invention that may be patented as utility patents are computer software and biotechnology products. Recent court decisions allow computer software to be protected as machines, articles of manufacture, composition of matter, or processes. Biotechnology products involve subject matter relating to life—transgenic animals, for example, or amino acid sequences or genetic sequences. One court decision considered a new bacterium that broke down crude oil to be patentable as a composition of matter or article of manufacture.

To qualify for a utility patent, an invention must be novel, useful, and nonobvious. Novelty means that an invention must not have been known or used previously by someone in the United States or published or patented previously anywhere in the world.

To be considered useful, an invention must work, solve the problem it was

In 1959 patent certificates are displayed on the wall at the Bristol Labs in Syracuse, New York. The display shows patents from many different countries for many of the same compounds. Multiple patents may be necessary for international production and distribution.

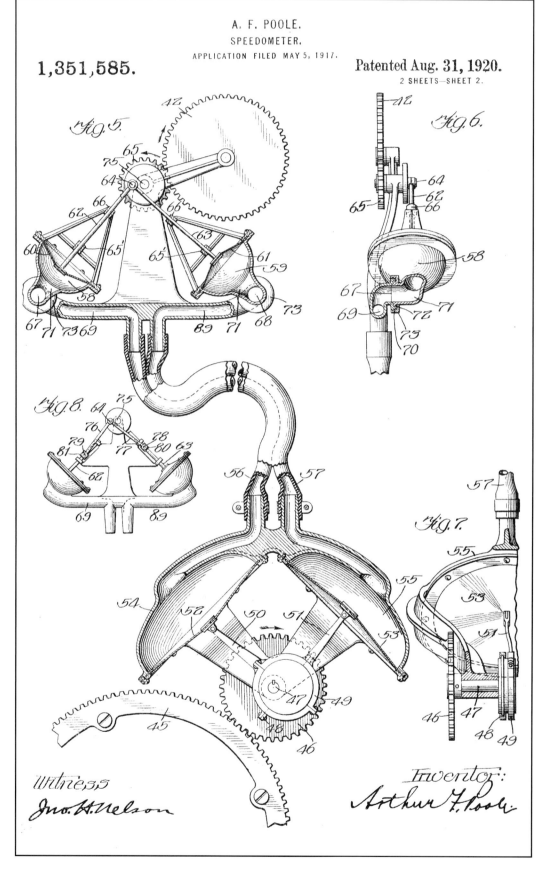

A. F. POOLE.
SPEEDOMETER.
APPLICATION FILED MAY 5, 1917.

Patent applications are accompanied by technical drawings that illustrate the mechanics of the invention. This is one of several illustrations that accompanied a patent application for a magnetic speedometer for automobiles; inventor Arthur F. Poole filed the application in 1917 and the patent was granted in 1920.

designed to solve, and provide some benefit to society. Most inventions meet the usefulness requirement, although questions of interpretation do arise regarding its meaning. Some people believe, incorrectly, that an invention must be commercially successful to be useful. An invention does not have to be highly marketable or have outstanding performance characteristics to satisfy the usefulness requirement. If an invention is regarded as harmful to society, then the usefulness requirement is not met. For example, in 1897 a new invention known as a slot machine was considered harmful to society.

Nonobviousness is the most critical test for an item to be patented. An invention is not obvious if a person of ordinary skill in the field fails to deduce it from the prior art (public knowledge, prior publications, etc.). This area is often a major source of disagreement between patent applicants and patent examiners. In ruling on disputes arising from these disagreements, courts consider several factors, including whether an invention would be a commercial success; whether it successfully addresses some long-felt but unmet need; and whether it is something others have tried but failed to develop.

Design Patents

A design patent protects the ornamental aspects of an article, or how the article looks. The design of an object may entail its configuration or shape; its surface ornamentation; and both its shape and surface ornamentation. However, a design patent does not protect the functional aspects of an invention.

A design patent consists in part of a series of drawings or photographs showing the ornamental features of an object. A design patent also includes a description of the object and its ornamental features. If drawings include too much detail, then somebody looking for a way to violate (infringe) the patent may have an easy task. The infringer could perhaps omit some small detail and contend that his or her invention is something new, falling outside the scope of the prior patent.

To qualify for a design patent, an invention must be novel and nonobvious. Such requirements are met if the shape, configuration, or surface ornamentation of the invention differs from and is not obvious in light of what is known publicly. Design patents remain in force for 14 years from the patent issue date.

An invention may receive both a design and a utility patent. The design patent protects the appearance of the article and the utility patent protects its functions. Examples of inventions that have been protected with both kinds of patents are tire treads, footwear, and flatware.

Plant Patents

The law also provides for the granting of a patent to anyone who has invented or discovered and asexually reproduced any distinct, new variety of plant. Asexually propagated plants are those reproduced by means other than seeding, for example, by the rooting of cuttings. Plant patents give the owner the right to exclude others from asexually reproducing the plant or selling or using the plant so reproduced.

Patents 1980 to 2000 (in thousands)					
	1980	1985	1990	1995	2000
Patent applications					
Inventions	104.3	117.0	164.6	212.4	295.9
Designs	7.8	9.6	11.3	15.4	18.3
Botanical plants	0.2	0.2	0.4	0.5	0.8
Reissues	0.6	0.3	0.5	0.6	NA
Total	113.0	127.1	176.7	228.8	NA
Patents issued					
Inventions	61.8	71.7	90.4	101.4	157.5
Individuals	13.8	12.9	17.3	17.4	22.4
U.S. corporations	27.7	31.2	36.1	44.0	70.9
U.S. government	1.2	1.1	1.0	1.0	0.9
Foreign (corporations and governments)	19.1	26.4	36.0	39.1	63.3
Designs	3.9	5.1	8.0	11.7	17.4
Botanical plants	0.1	0.2	0.3	0.4	0.5
Reissues	0.3	0.3	0.4	0.3	0.5
Total	66.2	77.3	99.2	113.8	176.0

NA = Not available.
Note: Covers patents issued to citizens of the United States and residents of foreign countries.
Source: U.S. Patent and Trademark Office.

Obtaining a Patent

To obtain a patent, an applicant submits a patent application to the U.S. Patent and Trademark Office. The application consists of a specification and claims, drawings (when appropriate), an oath or declaration by the applicant, and the filing fee. The specification is a written, technical description of the invention. The claims are one-sentence statements highlighting what it is that the inventor claims as an invention; these claims determine the property rights conferred by a patent. The drawings show features of the invention. Most mechanical and electrical patents have drawings, while most chemical and process patents do not. The specification, along with the drawings, must set forth the manner and process of making and using the invention. The oath or declaration is a statement by the applicant, asserting that he or she believes him- or herself to be the original inventor of the subject matter of the application.

After an application has been filed, it is assigned to a patent examiner who specializes in the subject matter of the application. The examiner does an initial study of the application to determine whether it follows Patent Office rules. One such rule is that each application may cover only one invention.

If the application passes the initial screening, the examiner does a detailed analysis for patentability. This includes a "prior art" search of all U.S. patents, foreign patents, and technical publications in the field to determine whether the subject matter is novel and nonobvious to those skilled in the field. After the prior art search, the patent examiner rules on the application and sends

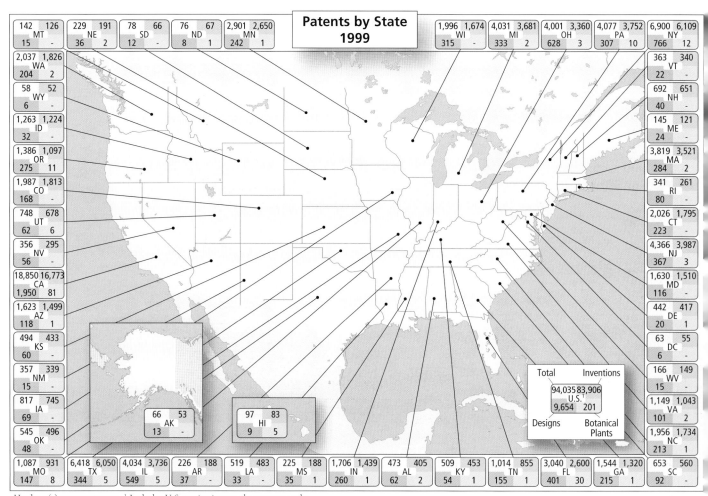

Patents by State 1999

Hyphen (-) represents zero. [1] Includes U.S. territories not shown separately.
Note: Includes only U. S. patents granted to residents of the United States and territories.
Source: U.S. Patent and Trademark Office, Technology Assessment and Forecast Database.

Dr. Ananda Chakrabarty poses in front of the U.S. Supreme Court. He was the first scientist to receive a patent on a life-form that resulted from his experiments with a recombinant-DNA-created oil-spill-eating bacteria. A 1983 Supreme Court decision validated the issuance of patents on life-forms created in the lab.

this decision, in writing, to the applicant or his patent lawyer or agent. If the application is denied, the applicant is provided time to ask for reconsideration of their applications.

After a reconsideration, the examiner's decision is again sent in writing to the applicant. Usually the second decision is final; however, if the second decision is

Software Patents

Patents are an important part of any technology corporation's property; software companies are especially reliant on patents. Software creation requires a significant investment of programming time and talent; however, it does not require the infrastructure needed by, for example, an automobile manufacturer. New software producers have relatively few barriers to entering the market and producing software applications. Therefore, the industry has attempted to find means of enforcing ownership over certain software processes.

Initially, patents appeared to offer little protection to computer programmers. A Supreme Court decision in 1972, *Gottschalk v. Benson*, determined that a computer algorithm was not subject to patent protection. Computer algorithms are procedures a programmer creates to perform particular tasks. A method for more quickly sorting a list of names into alphabetic order, for example, would be considered an algorithm. The Court determined that algorithms are more like mathematical formulas, abstract ideas, or natural laws: they are discovered rather than invented.

Gottschalk effectively made software unpatentable; however, the Court opened the door a bit to software patents almost a decade later in *Diamond v. Diehr*. The Court still maintained that many kinds of software were not patentable, but stated at the same time that the mere inclusion of a mathematical formula or an algorithm did not mean that an invention could not be patented. This position was cemented for software in *Whelan v. Jaslow* in 1986. This warming to software patents was further reinforced in the 1998 *State Street v. Signature* case, whose ruling did away with the exclusion of "business process" patents, allowing processes for services and sales techniques, which had become increasingly important on the Internet, to be patented.

Since the *State Street* case, a number of software patents have come under harsh criticism. In a few cases, the patents have even been reexamined and overturned. Some of these patents, if enforced, would make the World Wide Web impossible. British Telecommunications, for example, has attempted to enforce an older patent that appears to give it ownership over the idea of hyperlinking, and Unisys has begun to enforce its patent on the GIF picture-file format. Amazon.com's patents for "one-click" shopping (ordering and paying for a product with a single mouse click on a hyperlink) and for affiliate advertising have been criticized by many in the software industry.

Some, like members of MIT's League for Programming Freedom and Harvard University Law School professor Lawrence Lessig, see the rise of software patents as impeding innovation in software design. According to those who argue against software patents, many patents are used as leverage between large corporations, which force one another to share the use of a collection of patents to mutual benefit. As a result, individual programmers or small companies are unable to compete without worrying about infringing on one of the thousands of existing software patents. On the other hand, some believe that companies that invest in the research to create new software should be able to reap the benefits of that research.

—*Alexander Halavais*

An inventor who wishes to obtain patent protection in countries other than the United States must apply for a patent in each of the other countries. Almost every country has its own patent law, and a person desiring a patent in a particular country must make an application for patent in that country.

The Paris Convention for the Protection of Industrial Property is a treaty relating to patents that is adhered to by 140 countries, including the United States. The treaty provides that each signator guarantees to the citizens of other countries the same rights in patent matters that it gives to its own citizens. On the basis of a regular patent application filed in one of the member countries, the applicant may, within a certain time, apply for protection in all the other member nations.

Patent infringement occurs when any person or business makes, uses, or sells a patented invention without permission. The patent holder has redress and can file a civil lawsuit in any federal district court asking for damages and an injunction to prevent further infringement. Any district court decision may be appealed to a circuit court of appeals; in some cases, appeals reach the U.S. Supreme Court. Patent holders must mark their invented products as patented; failure to do so may prevent them from obtaining money damages in an infringement suit.

Further Reading

Branscomb, Anne Wells. *Who Owns Information? From Privacy to Public Access*. New York: BasicBooks, 1994.

Gordon, T., and A. Cookfair. *Patent Fundamentals for Scientists and Engineers*. 2nd ed. New York: Lewis Publishers, 2000.

Lessig, Lawrence. "Patent Problems." *Industry Standard* (January 2000).

Nichols, K. *Inventing Software: The Rise of Computer-Related Patents*. Westport, Conn.: Quorum Publishers, 1998.

Rivette, Kevin G., and David Kline. *Rembrandts in the Attic: Unlocking the Hidden Value of Patents*. Boston: Harvard Business School Press, 2000.

Shulman, Seth. *Owning the Future*. Boston: Houghton Mifflin, 1999.

—*Carl Pacini*

negative, the applicant may appeal to the U.S. Patent Office Board of Appeals, a judicial body within the Patent Office. Adverse decisions from the Board of Appeals can be reviewed by the Court of Custom and Patent Appeals or by the district court of the District of Columbia.

Pay Equity

Pay equity refers to efforts to ensure that men and women are paid the same for similar work. In the United States, 99 percent of women will work for pay at some point in their lives, earning about 74 percent of what men earn, or $26 less for every $100 worth of work. On an average, a working woman in the United States makes $13,087 less than a working man every year, according to the U.S. Census Bureau. Over a woman's working life she will earn nearly half a million dollars less than a man. Although this wage gap has narrowed, some experts believe part of that trend is the result of a decrease in men's real wages as well as an increase in women's.

In 1900 women constituted less than 18 percent of the paid workforce; by 1950 they were slightly less than 30 percent; by 2000, 48 percent. Although women have always worked, they have not always been—and are not always—paid for their work. Throughout history, "women's work" was to make life livable for their families. Even if, as in the case of farmers' wives, little difference existed in the actual work, her role was seen as supportive. Even today, much of the work done by women is unpaid, including agricultural work and child care; estimates are that women worldwide are not paid for as much as 66 percent of the work they do.

In the second half of the twentieth century, numerous forces converged that resulted in women's earnings becoming more similar to men's. The feminist movement of the late 1960s enabled women to enter the workforce in larger numbers and gain valuable and more highly compensated skills. Women are also getting more education than they were in the past, enabling them to get higher-paying jobs. Large-scale economic changes have made women's entry into the workforce necessary, as families are no longer able to thrive on just one salary. In addition, the U.S. economy has shifted away from manufacturing businesses toward service-oriented businesses, which open up opportunities for women to have longer and higher-paying careers.

Two laws protect U.S. workers against wage discrimination. The Equal Pay Act of 1963 prohibits unequal pay for equal or "substantially equal" work performed by men and women. Title VII of the Civil Rights Act of 1964 prohibits wage discrimination on the basis of race, color, sex, religion, or national origin. A division of the United States Department of Labor, the Equal Employment Opportunity Commission (EEOC), was established by Title VII of the Civil Rights Act of 1964 and began operating on July 2, 1965. The EEOC is responsible for enforcing these laws. Anyone can file a complaint with the EEOC about discrimination by an employer.

The gap between women and men's wages, while still significant, has narrowed substantially since the signing of the Equal Pay Act. The gap between men and women's wages

See also:
Civil Rights Legislation; Compensation; Equal Employment Opportunity Commission; Women in the Workforce.

Median Annual Earnings of Full-Time, Year-Round Workers 1980 to 2001 (in adjusted 2001 dollars)		
Year	Male	Female
1980	38,979	22,946
1981	38,514	22,521
1982	37,936	23,111
1983	37,797	23,716
1984	38,852	24,165
1985	39,324	24,785
1986	39,952	25,305
1987	39,533	25,445
1988	39,149	25,620
1989	39,347	26,086
1990	37,929	26,329
1991	38,361	26,355
1992	38,152	26,700
1993	37,505	26,568
1994	37,333	26,729
1995	37,109	26,427
1996	37,031	27,139
1997	38,706	27,860
1998	39,231	28,462
1999	39,565	28,322
2000	39,955	28,864
2001	39,834	29,930

Source: U.S. Bureau of the Census, Historical Income Tables—People, http://www.census.gov/hhes/income/histinc/p38a.html (March 3, 2003).

Jobs that are perceived as "women's work," such as waitressing, tend to pay less than jobs that are considered "men's work."

is often measured by calculating the ratio of women's to men's median pay. During the 1950s and 1960s, for example, women's median wages were about 60 percent of men's wages. For every dollar a man earned, a woman earned 60 cents. Women's earnings rose in the 1970s and 1980s and reached about 70 percent of men's earnings in 1990.

However, studies have shown that when the percentage of women rises in a particular occupation—when it starts to be seen as "women's work"—wages in that occupation begin to fall. Jobs in which 70 percent or more of the workers are women usually pay less than jobs that are balanced between genders or jobs that are predominantly male. Both the men and the women in those lower-paying, "women's" jobs are disadvantaged.

Salaries are not the only means of determining the pay equity of women compared with men. Increasingly, the benefits that do—or do not—come with employment are

Median Weekly Earnings by Occupational Group 2000	Male	Female
Managerial and professional	$994	$709
Technical, sales, and administrative support	$1,014	$452
Service	$414	$316
Operators, fabricators, and laborers	$487	$351
Farming, forestry, and fishing	$347	$294

Source: U.S. Bureau of the Census, *Statistical Abstract of the United States:* 2001, http://www.census.gov/prod/2002pubs/01statab/labor.pdf (March 3, 2003).

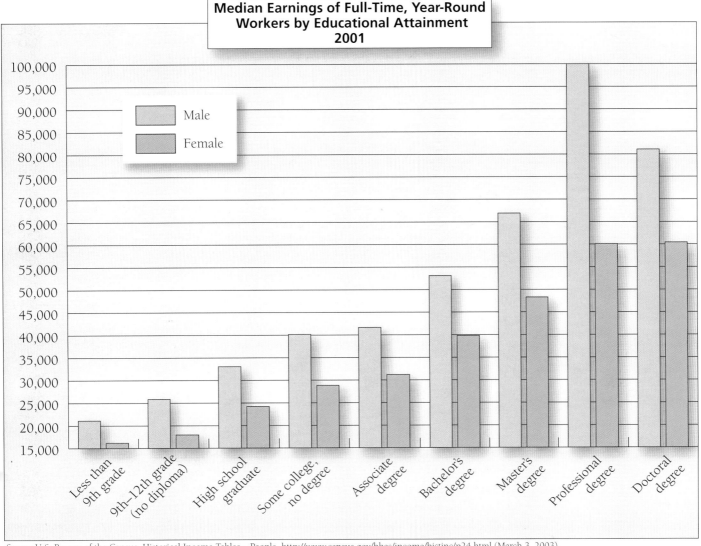

Median Earnings of Full-Time, Year-Round Workers by Educational Attainment 2001

Legend:
- Male
- Female

Y-axis values: 15,000 / 20,000 / 25,000 / 30,000 / 35,000 / 40,000 / 45,000 / 50,000 / 55,000 / 60,000 / 65,000 / 70,000 / 75,000 / 80,000 / 85,000 / 90,000 / 95,000 / 100,000

X-axis categories: Less than 9th grade / 9th–12th grade (no diploma) / High school graduate / Some college, no degree / Associate degree / Bachelor's degree / Master's degree / Professional degree / Doctoral degree

Source: U.S. Bureau of the Census, Historical Income Tables—People, http://www.census.gov/hhes/income/histinc/p24.html (March 3, 2003).

very important. For instance, in 1993, 62 percent of male workers in the private sector received health insurance, while only 51 percent of female workers did. Forty-six percent of male workers in the United States are covered under an employer's pension plan, but only 39 percent of women. Fourteen percent of working women have no sick leave and risk having their pay cut for missing even one day of work.

Pay inequity exists in all professions. Women lawyers and doctors in the United States earn hundreds of dollars less a week than males in those professions. Even in traditionally female-dominated jobs, women do not receive equal pay. Although 95 percent of nurses are female, they earn $30 less a week than the 5 percent of male nurses.

Waitresses' average weekly earnings are $50 less than that of waiters. Efforts to close the remaining gap in pay focus on providing women with the education and training to enable them to get jobs that pay higher wages and to improve the ability of women to file discrimination complaints.

Further Reading

Blau, Francine D., Marianne A. Ferber, and Anne E. Winkler. *The Economics of Women, Men, and Work.* 4th ed. Upper Saddle River, N.J.: Prentice-Hall, 2001.

Goldin, Claudia. *Understanding the Gender Gap.* New York: Oxford University Press, 1990.

Gunderson, Morley. *Comparable Worth and Gender Discrimination: An International Perspective.* Geneva: International Labour Office, 1994.

—*Carl Haacke and Jo Lynn Southard*

The W-4 form opposite is used to calculate the taxes to be deducted from employee paychecks.

Payroll

Payroll is a company's accounting of what it pays its employees. A payroll department is staffed by a group of people responsible for producing accurate paychecks and for paying employee-related taxes to the appropriate government authorities. The payroll department performs both an accounting function and an administrative function. Payroll accounting handles the numbers—calculating wages, documenting the cost of employees for the company's internal balance sheets, and processing year-end wage statements for tax purposes. Payroll administration tracks employee information affecting wages and submits payroll reports and taxes collected by the various government tax agencies.

Calculating Wages

An employee's first contact with payroll occurs the first day on the job. A new employee typically gets a sheaf of forms to fill out, including several that go directly to the payroll department. The W-4 form is used to calculate an employee's withholding for tax purposes. The number of deductions entered on this form is used by the payroll department to calculate the amount of money that will be taken from the person's income each pay period and sent to the Internal Revenue Service (IRS). If the company operates in a state or local area that levies taxes on income, then payroll uses the number of deductions on the W-4 to calculate the state and local taxes withheld, too. The payroll department is also responsible for garnisheeing wages when ordered by a court of law.

Another form that goes directly to payroll is the direct deposit form. Employees often can choose to have their paychecks deposited directly into their bank accounts each pay period. This is advantageous for both the employer and the employee. The employer saves the cost of having checks pass through its bank account and the employee need not get the check to the bank. Payroll still provides a pay stub for each employee showing the amount of the direct deposit and all the deductions taken for that period.

Another form that affects payroll is the benefits enrollment form. Most benefits are paid for, in part, by employees. The payments are deducted from employees' income each pay period. For example, companies usually charge for the various kinds of insurance: medical, dental, accidental death, and additional life insurance above what the company offers. Deductions for retirement plans are also noted on the benefits enrollment form. Some companies offer other voluntary deductions, such as flexible spending accounts (FSAs) for future medical or child care expenses.

Because of deductions the salary earned is not the salary paid. Some of the money can be recouped at tax time if the employee has had more money withheld than needed. However, other taxes—those collected for Medicare and social security (FICA)—are paid to the government permanently.

After receiving the employee's forms, the payroll department balances those against income. Income is calculated according to the employee's hiring arrangement and the number and kind of hours worked. Payroll tracks time on the job and time off the job to calculate income. Time on the job is the time spent working. Time off the job can be vacation time, sick leave, family leave, jury duty, and so on. Some time off may be paid, some may not.

An employee can be hourly, salaried, contract labor, or temporary. An hourly employee is paid a set amount for each hour worked, for example, $8.00 per hour. Hourly employees are typically paid more for overtime, usually time and a half (one and one-half times the regular hourly wage). Salaried employees are paid a set amount of money, for example, $25,000 per year, regardless of the number of hours worked. The $25,000 would be divided equally among the pay periods. Another distinction that affects payroll is that of part-time or full-time. In general, only full-time employees

A dependent is usually a child—but can also be a sibling or parent in some circumstances—who is financially supported by the taxpayer.

A head of household is someone who is unmarried and paying more than 50 percent of the costs of keeping up a home for him or herself and for dependents.

Form W-4 (2002)

Purpose. Complete Form W-4 so your employer can withhold the correct Federal income tax from your pay. Because your tax situation may change, you may want to refigure your withholding each year.

Exemption from withholding. If you are exempt, complete only lines 1, 2, 3, 4, and 7 and sign the form to validate it. Your exemption for 2002 expires February 16, 2003. See **Pub. 505,** Tax Withholding and Estimated Tax.

Note: *You cannot claim exemption from withholding if* **(a)** *your income exceeds $750 and includes more than $250 of unearned income (e.g., interest and dividends) and* **(b)** *another person can claim you as a dependent on their tax return.*

Basic instructions. If you are not exempt, complete the **Personal Allowances Worksheet** below. The worksheets on page 2 adjust your withholding allowances based on itemized deductions, certain credits, adjustments to

income, or two-earner/two-job situations. Complete all worksheets that apply. **However, you may claim fewer (or zero) allowances.**

Head of household. Generally, you may claim head of household filing status on your tax return only if you are unmarried and pay more than 50% of the costs of keeping up a home for yourself and your dependent(s) or other qualifying individuals. See line **E** below.

Tax credits. You can take projected tax credits into account in figuring your allowable number of withholding allowances. Credits for child or dependent care expenses and the child tax credit may be claimed using the **Personal Allowances Worksheet** below. See **Pub. 919, How Do I Adjust My Tax Withholding?** for information on converting your other credits into withholding allowances.

Nonwage income. If you have a large amount of nonwage income, such as interest or dividends, consider making estimated tax payments using Form **1040-ES,** Estimated Tax for Individuals. Otherwise, you may owe additional tax.

Two earners/two jobs. If you have a working spouse or more than one job, figure the total number of allowances you are entitled to claim on all jobs using worksheets from only one Form W-4. Your withholding usually will be most accurate when all allowances are claimed on the Form W-4 for the highest paying job and zero allowances are claimed on the others.

Nonresident alien. If you are a nonresident alien, see the **Instructions for Form 8233** before completing this Form W-4.

Check your withholding. After your Form W-4 takes effect, use Pub. 919 to see how the dollar amount you are having withheld compares to your projected total tax for 2002. See Pub. 919, especially if you used the **Two-Earner/Two-Job Worksheet** on page 2 and your earnings exceed $125,000 (Single) or $175,000 (Married).

Recent name change? If your name on line 1 differs from that shown on your social security card, call 1-800-772-1213 for a new social security card.

Personal Allowances Worksheet (Keep for your records.)

A Enter "1" for **yourself** if no one else can claim you as a **dependent** . . . . A _____

B Enter "1" if: { You are single and have only one job; or / You are married, have only one job, and your spouse does not work; or / Your wages from a second job or your spouse's wages (or the total of both) are $1,000 or less. } . . . B _____

C Enter "1" for your **spouse.** But, you may choose to enter "-0-" if you are married and have either a working spouse or more than one job. (Entering "-0-" may help you avoid having too little tax withheld.) . . . . C _____

D Enter number of **dependents** (other than your spouse or yourself) you will claim on your tax return . . . . D _____

E Enter "1" if you will file as **head of household** on your tax return (see conditions under **Head of household** above) . E _____

F Enter "1" if you have at least $1,500 of **child or dependent care expenses** for which you plan to claim a credit . F _____
(**Note:** *Do not include child support payments. See* **Pub. 503,** *Child and Dependent Care Expenses, for details.*)

G **Child Tax Credit** (including additional child tax credit):
• If your total income will be between $15,000 and $42,000 ($20,000 and $65,000 if married), enter "1" for each eligible child plus **1 additional** if you have three to five eligible children or **2 additional** if you have six or more eligible children.
• If your total income will be between $42,000 and $80,000 ($65,000 and $115,000 if married), enter "1" if you have one or two eligible children, "2" if you have three eligible children, "3" if you have four eligible children, or "4" if you have five or more eligible children. . G _____

H Add lines A through G and enter total here. **Note:** *This may be different from the number of exemptions you claim on your tax return.* . H _____

For accuracy, complete all worksheets that apply.
• If you plan to **itemize or claim adjustments to income** and want to reduce your withholding, see the **Deductions and Adjustments Worksheet** on page 2.
• If you have **more than one job** or are **married and you and your spouse both work** and the combined earnings from all jobs exceed $35,000, see the **Two-Earner/Two-Job Worksheet** on page 2 to avoid having too little tax withheld.
• If **neither** of the above situations applies, **stop here** and enter the number from line H on line 5 of Form W-4 below.

Cut here and give Form W-4 to your employer. Keep the top part for your records.

Form **W-4**
Department of the Treasury
Internal Revenue Service

Employee's Withholding Allowance Certificate

For Privacy Act and Paperwork Reduction Act Notice, see page 2.

OMB No. 1545-0010

2002

1 Type or print your first name and middle initial | Last name

| 2 Your social security number

Home address (number and street or rural route)

City or town, state, and ZIP code

3 ☐ Single ☐ Married ☐ Married, but withhold at higher Single rate.
Note: *If married, but legally separated, or spouse is a nonresident alien, check the "Single" box.*

4 If your last name differs from that on your social security card, check here. You must call 1-800-772-1213 for a new card. ☐

5 Total number of allowances you are claiming (from line **H** above **or** from the applicable worksheet on page 2) | 5 _____

6 Additional amount, if any, you want withheld from each paycheck | 6 $ _____

7 I claim exemption from withholding for 2002, and I certify that I meet **both** of the following conditions for exemption:
• Last year I had a right to a refund of **all** Federal income tax withheld because I had **no** tax liability **and**
• This year I expect a refund of **all** Federal income tax withheld because I expect to have **no** tax liability.
If you meet both conditions, write "Exempt" here . . . . | 7 _____

Under penalties of perjury, I certify that I am entitled to the number of withholding allowances claimed on this certificate, or I am entitled to claim exempt status.

Employee's signature
(Form is not valid unless you sign it.) ▶ _____ Date ▶ _____

8 Employer's name and address (Employer: Complete lines 8 and 10 only if sending to the IRS.) | 9 Office code (optional) | 10 Employer identification number

Cat. No. 10220Q

Some jobs require that employees keep time cards that are "punched in" on arrival and "punched out" upon departure, so that hours of work can be calculated automatically.

qualify for full company benefits. Payroll must determine which employees are eligible for which benefits.

Sample Direct Deposit Form

Widgets International, Ltd.
Automatic Salary Deposit Application

I authorize Widgets International to automatically deposit the amount of my monthly payroll check into the bank account listed below. This authorization is to remain in effect until Widgets International receives written notification of termination from me.

Signature *Mark Wood*   Date *April 23, 2003*

Bank Name: *Northeast Savings and Loan*

Bank Routing and Transit Number: *445299101*

Type of Bank Account: Checking   ⟨Savings⟩

Bank Account Number: *22200127*

Paying Taxes

The payroll department performs two functions related to taxes. The first is that of holding payroll taxes in trust for the government. Payroll taxes, or income taxes collected from employees on behalf of the government, are typically deposited into a separate checking account from the company's business account. State and local taxes are paid periodically; federal taxes, depending on the amount collected, are paid to the IRS every month or semi-monthly. The employer must also give an accurate accounting of its employees' income and tax-related deductions. The IRS is not very forgiving of late payments as the money really belongs to the government, not the company making the payment to the IRS. Late payments incur both stiff penalties and interest.

The second function is to pay the government for taxes the company owes on its employees. Employers are required to pay half of the social security tax for all employees. Payroll tracks and pays the 7.5 percent that the company owes the IRS on each

Sample Payroll Statement

Employee	ID	Social Security	Status	Exemptions/Allowances
John F. Smith	1402	000-00-0000	Single	Federal: $500.00
				State: $150.00

Hire Date	Period Start	Period End	Pay Date
01/4/00	01/01/03	01/15/03	01/15/03

Earnings	Current	Year to Date
Salary	4,000.00	4,000.00
Bonus	1,000.00	1,000.00
Total Gross	5,000.00	5,000.00
Taxes		
Federal Income Tax	500.00	500.00
Social Security (FICA)	225.00	225.00
Federal Medicare	50.00	50.00
Connecticut Income Tax	150.00	150.00
Total	925.00	925.00
PreTax Deductions		
Medical Plan	60.00	60.00
401(k) Savings Plan-Matched	75.00	75.00
Total	135.00	135.00
Net Pay	3940.00	

employee. Contract workers and consultants are usually considered self-employed, so they pay the full 15 percent on their individual tax returns.

Reporting

Payroll provides management with valuable information in reports. Payroll reports calculate the cost of employing each person in terms of salary, benefits, and taxes. Depending upon whether the company is taxed by state and local entities, taxes alone can cost the company up to 20 percent of a person's salary. Benefits also cost the company money, thus some companies prefer to hire independent contractors. Contractors are usually paid a higher salary than are regular employees because they pay for their own benefits, insurance, and taxes.

Payroll generates reports that calculate the cost of each employee. These reports can be used to track labor distribution throughout the company, to control labor costs overall or by project, and to alert management about any staffing problems. Payroll reports can also be used to show inequity in pay and to help develop pay scales for various kinds of jobs and levels of experience.

Further Reading

American Payroll Association, Legal editorial staff. *Federal Payroll Tax Laws & Regulations.* New York: American Payroll Association, 2000.

Giove, Frank C. *Payroll Accounting: A Complete Guide to Payroll.* 2nd ed. Boston: Houghton Mifflin College, 2001.

O'Toole, Michael P. *The Payroll Source.* New York: American Payroll Association, 2000.

—Stephanie Buckwalter

Perkins, Frances

1882–1965
Secretary of Labor, 1933–1945

Frances Perkins was a social reformer, champion of working people, and the first woman to serve in the U.S. Cabinet. She was secretary of labor from 1933 to 1945, during the presidency of Franklin Delano Roosevelt. "Madame Secretary," as Perkins preferred to be addressed, served in Roosevelt's cabinet during much of the Great Depression. Describing her mission she said, "I came to Washington to work for God, FDR and the millions of forgotten, plain common workingmen."

Early Activism

Perkins, born in 1882, was raised in Worcester, Massachusetts. Her career as a reformer began at Mount Holyoke College, where she helped to establish a chapter of the National Consumers' League, an organization dedicated to the abolition of sweatshops and child labor. In 1902 she earned a bachelor's degree in chemistry and physics. After graduation, she did social work for the Episcopal Church and taught high school chemistry. While teaching at a school in Chicago, she became interested in Hull House, an institution that offered social services to inner-city poor. She lived and worked at Hull House for six months, inspecting tenements and sweatshops and becoming acquainted with social workers in the area.

In 1907 Perkins gave up teaching science and enrolled in the University of Pennsylvania, where she studied economics and sociology and continued to do social work. She moved to New York in 1909, where she investigated child malnutrition in some of the city's poorest neighborhoods, and in 1910 received her master's degree in sociology and economics from Columbia University. That same year she became executive secretary of the New York City Consumer's League, where she lobbied for fire prevention in factories, the 54-hour maximum workweek for women, and bakery sanitation.

Perkins began working with trade unionists and New York State Assembly leaders to lobby for industrial and labor regulation. In 1919 Al Smith, the governor of New York, appointed her to serve on the Industrial Commission of the State of New York, and in 1926 she became its chairwoman, where her duties included administration of the Workmen's Compensation Act. When Franklin Roosevelt became governor of New York in 1929, he appointed Perkins to the job of industrial commissioner, the head of the state labor department. In this post, which she held until 1933, Perkins emphasized workmen's

Frances Perkins in 1940.

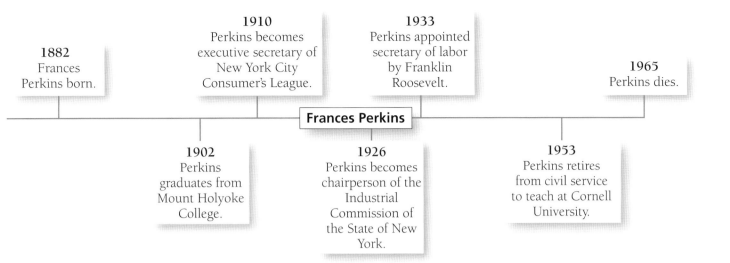

1882
Frances
Perkins born.

1910
Perkins becomes
executive secretary of
New York City
Consumer's League.

1933
Perkins appointed
secretary of labor
by Franklin
Roosevelt.

1965
Perkins dies.

Frances Perkins

1902
Perkins
graduates from
Mount Holyoke
College.

1926
Perkins becomes
chairperson of the
Industrial
Commission of
the State of New
York.

1953
Perkins retires
from civil service
to teach at Cornell
University.

compensation, unemployment insurance, shorter workweeks, factory inspection, and the abolition of child labor. In this capacity she forged an excellent working relationship with Roosevelt.

Perkins regarded herself as a nonpartisan reformer and for many years avoided affiliating with a political party. In 1920, however, she registered as a Democrat, despite the influence of her staunchly conservative parents, who were Republicans.

Perkins was more than familiar with surprising her parents—and the general public—with what a woman in the first half of the twentieth century could accomplish. "The accusation that I am a woman is incontrovertible," she once said. She shielded her personal life so completely that most Americans did not know she was married and had a daughter; in public life she remained "Miss Perkins." She was also fond of recalling that, "Being a woman has only bothered me in climbing trees." Nevertheless, she encountered much hostility from both labor and industrial leaders during her tenure as secretary of labor.

*Frances Perkins greets
President Franklin D. Roosevelt,
circa 1933.*

Perkins, Frances   995

Perkins and the New Deal

When Roosevelt became president in 1933, an estimated 13 million Americans were out of work—25 percent of the workforce. To stimulate recovery, Perkins proposed: immediate federal aid to the states for direct unemployment relief; an extensive program of public works projects (the building of roads, sewer systems, dams, and so forth, that would benefit the country while employing workers); a study that would lead to the establishment of federal laws mandating minimum wages, maximum hours, unemployment and old-age insurance; the abolition of child labor; and the creation of a federal employment service.

Through various legislation, including the National Industrial Recovery Act of 1933, the Fair Labor Standards Act, and the Social Security Act—largely considered her greatest contribution to social reform—many of Perkins's proposals were realized while she was secretary of labor. These and many other initiatives were informally referred to as the New Deal, recalling a phrase the president used in his 1932 election campaign that was, according to Perkins's writings, a general idea that the "little man" would be dealt a better hand in life.

Despite her role in contributing to the crafting of these and other important laws, Perkins was often harshly criticized. She was labeled ineffective at mediating labor disputes, was unable to bring about the unification of the American Federation of Labor and the Congress of Industrial Organizations (the merger occurred in 1955), and ultimately failed to create a national minimum wage. She was alternately accused of being a communist and a mere bureaucrat. Perkins survived several attempts by conservatives to remove her from office.

Perkins served as secretary of labor until July 1945, three months after Roosevelt died in office. President Harry Truman then appointed her to the Civil Service Commission, where she remained through 1953. After retiring from government, Perkins wrote books, lectured on labor and industrial topics at several universities, and

In 1935 Perkins surveys the work on the Golden Gate Bridge, discussing its progress with project foremen.

Social Insurance for the United States
(Excerpt)

I have been asked to speak to you tonight on the administration's program for economic security which is now, as you know, before Congress. It seems to me that few legislative proposals have had as careful study, as thorough and conscientious deliberation as went into the preparation of these measures. The program now under consideration represents, I believe, a most significant step in our national development, a milestone in our progress toward the better-ordered society.

As I look back on the tragic years since 1929, it seems to me that we as a nation, not unlike some individuals, have been able to pass through a bitter experience to emerge with a newfound insight and maturity. We have had the courage to face our problems and find a way out. The heedless optimism of the boom years is past. We now stand ready to build the future with sanity and wisdom.

The process of recovery is not a simple one. We cannot be satisfied merely with makeshift arrangements which will tide us over the present emergencies. We must devise plans that will not merely alleviate the ills of today, but will prevent, as far as it is humanly possible to do so, their recurrence in the future. The task of recovery is inseparable from the fundamental task of social reconstruction. . . .

We cannot hope to accomplish [it] all in one bold stroke. To begin too ambitiously in the program of social security might very well result in errors which would entirely discredit this very necessary type of legislation. It is not amiss to note here that social legislation in European countries, begun some 25 years ago, is still in a developmental state and has been subjected to numerous changes as experience and changing conditions dictated.

It may come as a surprise to many of us that we in this country should be so far behind Europe in providing our citizens with those safeguards which assure a decent standard of living in both good times and bad, but the reasons are not far to seek. We are much younger than our European neighbors. Our abundant pioneer days are not very far behind us. With unlimited opportunities, in those days, for the individual who wished to take advantage of them, dependency seemed a reflection on the individual himself, rather than the result of social or economic conditions. There seemed little need for any systematic organized plan, such as has now become necessary.

It has taken the rapid industrialization of the last few decades, with its mass-production methods, to teach us that a man might become a victim of circumstances far beyond his control. . . . We have come to learn that the large majority of our citizens must have protection against the loss of income due to unemployment, old age, death of the breadwinners and disabling accident and illness, not only on humanitarian grounds, but in the interest of our national welfare. If we are to maintain a healthy economy and thriving production, we need to maintain the standard of living of the lower income groups in our population who constitute 90 percent of our purchasing power. . . .

The American program for economic security now before our Congress follows no single pattern. It is broader than social insurance, and does not attempt merely to copy a European model. Where other measures seemed more appropriate to our background or present situation, we have not hesitated to deviate from strict social insurance principles. In doing so we feel that we have recommended the measures which at this time seemed best calculated under our American conditions to protect individuals in the years immediately ahead from the hazards which might otherwise plunge them into destitution and dependency.

—Frances Perkins, national radio address, February 25, 1935

eventually became a visiting professor at Cornell University, where she continued to teach until two weeks before her death in 1965.

Despite the varied and often hostile reactions to Perkins during her 12 years in the Cabinet, history has remembered her well. The U.S. Labor Department building in Washington, D.C., is named after her, and she has been honored in the Labor Hall of Fame. Arthur J. Goldberg, one of Perkins's successors as secretary of labor, who later became an associate justice of the U.S. Supreme Court, said at the time of her death, "Under her wise and inspiring leadership, the Department of Labor came of age."

Further Reading

Kennedy, Susan Estabrook. "Frances Perkins." In *American National Biography*, Vol. 17. New York: Oxford University Press, 1999.

Mohr, Lillian Holmen. *Frances Perkins, That Woman in FDR's Cabinet!* Croton-on-Hudson, N.Y.: North River Press, 1979.

Perkins, Frances. *The Roosevelt I Knew.* New York: Viking Press, 1946.

—*Barbara Gerber*

See also:

Computer Industry;
Data Management;
Entrepreneurship;
General Motors; IBM.

Perot, H. Ross

1930–
Entrepreneur and politician

H. Ross Perot is a highly successful entrepreneur who transformed his company, Electronic Data Systems (EDS), from a one-man start-up to a multibillion-dollar corporate giant. Perot is perhaps even better known for his activities in public service and politics.

Perot was born on June 27, 1930, in Texarkana, Texas, to Ross and Lulu May Perot. He attended public schools in Texarkana, and he also attended Texarkana Junior College. Perot got started working by age seven, delivering newspapers and selling magazines, garden seeds, saddles, even horses and calves.

In 1949 Perot entered the United States Naval Academy. Before his graduation in 1953 he served as class president, battalion commander, and chairman of the honor committee. Perot then completed his military tour of duty, serving on board a naval destroyer and an aircraft carrier for four years. In 1956 he married Margot Birmingham, whom he had met while attending the Naval Academy. Perot was honorably discharged from the military in 1957, and he and his wife settled in Dallas.

In 1957 Perot began working as a salesman for International Business Machine Corporation (IBM), in its data processing division. In 1962 Birmingham lent Perot $1,000 from her earnings as a teacher so he could start EDS, a data processing company. Perot believed that future growth and earnings in the computer industry would be tied to software development, not to computer hardware. Perot took his company public (offered ownership shares for sale to the public) in 1968, earning Perot several hundred million dollars. His reputation for resourcefulness and bold action spread rapidly, and in 1969 U.S. government officials included Perot in a project for securing improved treatment for U.S. prisoners of war in Southeast Asia during the Vietnam War. Perot worked at this project until the end of American involvement in the war in 1973. For his contributions he was awarded the Medal for Distinguished Public Service, the highest civilian award conferred by the Department of Defense.

In 1979 Perot became involved once again in high-stakes, international negotiations. Two EDS employees had been taken hostage and imprisoned in Iran. Perot went to Iran and negotiated their release. Ken Follett later wrote a novel, *On Wings of Eagles* (1983), about the rescue mission, which also became the subject of a television miniseries.

Beginning in 1979 Perot involved himself in domestic politics. Appointed by the Texas state government to a War on Drugs Committee, Perot proposed five bills aimed at tightening restrictions on illegal drug operations to the state legislature; all five bills were eventually signed into law. In 1982, serving on another committee appointed to advise the Texas legislature, Perot led an effort to improve public

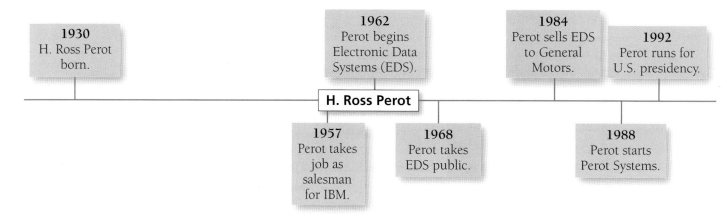

1930
H. Ross Perot born.

1957
Perot takes job as salesman for IBM.

1962
Perot begins Electronic Data Systems (EDS).

1968
Perot takes EDS public.

H. Ross Perot

1984
Perot sells EDS to General Motors.

1988
Perot starts Perot Systems.

1992
Perot runs for U.S. presidency.

education, proposing increased spending on the schools and also measures to raise academic standards.

In 1984 Perot sold EDS to General Motors (GM) for $2.5 billion. He became a member of the GM board of directors and GM's largest individual stockholder. Two years later, however, Perot resigned from the board, citing his disagreements with GM officials over the quality of their automobiles. He turned again to a business of his own in 1988, and created a new company. Perot Systems, which operates throughout the country, specializes in computer service.

In 1992 after some uncharacteristic vacillation, Perot ran for the U.S. presidency as an independent candidate sponsored by the Reform Party. He ran against Democrat Bill Clinton and Republican George H. W. Bush, the incumbent. Perot's down-to-earth manner and affection for folksy expressions such as "that dog won't hunt" endeared him to some voters and made him a figure of amusement to others. He lost to Bill Clinton but received 19 percent of the vote, and his candidacy raised many questions about the nation's two-party system. Polls indicated he took votes away from Bush and Clinton in about equal measure, and his influence—in capturing media attention and voter interest—was evident.

Perot continued his work with the Reform Party in the 1996 congressional elections; by 1996 he also was ready to try again for the presidency, competing this time against President Clinton and Republican challenger Bob Dole. The Reform Party, which focuses on campaign finance reform and balancing the budget, continued to draw attention as it brought its issues forward during the campaign. Perot attracted so much attention that Dole attempted to convince him to withdraw from the race and endorse the Republican ticket, but Perot dismissed the appeal. Perot, who had been very critical of Clinton, again lost to Clinton, this time garnering only 8 percent of the vote. Postelection polls showed that most Perot voters were less educated, poor, and generally

In 1969 H. Ross Perot watches as volunteers repackage Christmas gifts into 8,000 parcels for prisoners of war in North Vietnam.

pessimistic in comparison with other voters. Perot has continued to work with the Reform Party, although it was greatly weakened by his 1996 defeat. The party continues to advocate measures to restrict campaign contributions and reduce campaign costs by shortening the election cycle.

Over the years Perot has involved himself in a surprising range of philanthropic and humanitarian projects, donating more than $100 million to various charities. In 1984 he purchased the only copy of the Magna Carta (a charter signed by King John of England in 1215, guaranteeing

Perot, H. Ross   999

H. Ross Perot delivers a campaign speech in 1992.

some rights to English citizens) in existence outside of Great Britain. He lent the document to the National Archives in Washington, D.C., where it has been displayed alongside the U.S. Constitution and the Bill of Rights. Perot has received many awards, including the Sarnoff Award for contributions to the electronics industry, the Patrick Henry Award for outstanding service to the United States, and the Smithsonian Computerworld Award for contributions to the computer industry. His interests and achievements have consistently been exceptional.

In a world where people just tiptoe around life, live it to the fullest. Live it with zest. . . . In the words of Lech Walesa to our Congress, "Words are plentiful but deeds are precious." Now, in our country right now, if we had a pothole in the streets of a lot of our cities, we'd have a press conference on potholes. What we need in your generation is just get hot asphalt, get a shovel, fill the pothole, move on to the next one, skip the press conference. Right? That's action, not talk.

Always stand on principle. Don't worry about getting a broken nose. Fight for what you believe in even if it's unpopular. Don't worry about how things look and focus on how things really are. Do the right thing. Take the heat. Ignore the imagery and spin control that dominate our society today. When you foul up, just step up to the plate and say, I did it. That would be a refreshing change, right? Keep in mind your mistakes are painful for you but they're like skinned knees in little children. They're painful, they're superficial, they heal quickly and there's no better way to learn than from your honest mistakes. You've got to be involved. You've got to be in the ring.

—H. Ross Perot, address to 1995 graduating class of Port Huron Northern High School, Michigan

Further Reading

Brown, Gene. *H. Ross Perot: Texas Billionaire.* Vero Beach, Fla.: Rourke Enterprises, 1993.

Chiu, Tony. *Ross Perot in His Own Words.* New York: Warner Books, 1992.

Perot, H. Ross. *Ross Perot Speaks Out.* Rocklin, Calif.: Prima Publishing, 1992.

—*Karen Ayers*

Philip Morris Companies

Tobacco and food giant Philip Morris controls a number of international consumer goods companies but is probably best known for being the largest tobacco company in the world. Philip Morris is a holding company, owning majority stock in other big companies like Kraft Foods. Philip Morris is the tenth largest corporation in the United States; its revenues were close to $73 billion in 2002.

Tobacco has long been a staple of the U.S. economy; the cultivation of tobacco, a colonial cash crop in North America, began at Jamestown in the mid-seventeenth century. The invention of the cigarette in the early nineteenth century popularized smoking in both North America and Europe. Cigarettes began to be mass-produced in the United States around 1860, and after the U.S. Civil War (1861–1865) southern states, including Virginia and North Carolina, began supplying the rest of the country and Europe with tobacco.

In the mid-1800s Philip Morris opened a retail tobacco and cigar shop on Bond Street, in the heart of London. Morris began making cigarettes for sale in his shop in 1854. After Morris's death in 1873, his wife Margaret and brother Leopold took over the business. Leopold Morris bought Margaret's share in 1880 and took the company public the following year, renaming it Philip Morris & Company. Business was not good for Leopold, and creditors seized the company in 1894.

Majority control was sold to William Curtis Thomson and his family, who did a better job running the business. By 1901 Philip Morris & Company was successful enough to be appointed tobacconist to King Edward VII. With this boost in sales and publicity, the company incorporated in New York the following year. Ownership was split equally between the British and American partners. In 1919 a group of American stockholders, led by the company's American partners, acquired the company and incorporated in Virginia under the name Philip Morris & Company, Limited. It began manufacturing its own cigarettes in 1929 and went public in 1938.

Expanding the Company

The company grew steadily. Its signature Marlboro brand was the top-selling filtered cigarette in America in 1955 and the top-selling cigarette in the world by 1972. Around that time, the company began diversifying. In 1969 Philip Morris purchased Miller Brewing Company, the seventh largest brewer in the United States. Miller soon introduced new products: Miller Lite, the

See also:
Business Ethics; Liability.

Philip Morris Companies

1854 Philip Morris begins making cigarettes for sale in his London shop.

1901 Philip Morris appointed tobacconist for King Edward VII.

1938 Philip Morris goes public.

1955 Philip Morris's Marlboro brand is the top-selling cigarette in the United States.

1969 Philip Morris buys Miller Brewing Company.

1998 U.S. tobacco industry, including Philip Morris, agrees to pay $206 billion in tobacco-related claims.

2000 Philip Morris buys RJR Nabisco for $19 billion.

2002 Philip Morris changes its name to Altria Group. claims.

Processing cigarettes at a Philip Morris plant in Richmond, Virginia.

first low-calorie beer, and Miller Draft. Their popularity pushed the brewery into the number two spot by 1977.

Philip Morris acquired the soft-drink company Seven-Up in 1978 (sold in 1986) and General Foods Corporation in 1985. General Foods, purchased for $5.6 billion, was then the largest non-oil acquisition in U.S. history. That deal is also remembered for being the first time a U.S. company obtained most of the financing for an acquisition from banks outside the United States. Revenues and earnings grew tremendously, and in 1988 Philip Morris repeated the coup by acquiring Kraft Foods for $13.6 billion, setting a new record for the largest non-oil acquisition in U.S. history. The merged Kraft General Foods—renamed Kraft Foods in 1995—was the largest food company in the United States.

Philip Morris and its subsidiaries have since been buying up food companies around the world. Brazil's leading chocolate company, Industrias de Chocolate Lacta S.A., was purchased in 1996, Pabst and Stroh breweries in 1999, and a record $19 billion was spent to buy RJR Nabisco in 2000. By 2001 Philip Morris owned many of the world's favorite food brands and was the world's top cigarette maker, earning over $80 billion. Behind the image of Jello and Macaroni 'n' Cheese was a tobacco giant, with large potential liabilities related to the health risks of smoking.

Tobacco Controversy

One of the earliest lawsuits involving the smoking of tobacco was brought in 1954, when a Missouri smoker sued Philip Morris after losing his larynx to cancer. The case did not come to court until 1962, when it took the jury less than one hour to find in favor of the tobacco company. By then, tobacco companies had known for more than 10 years of the direct link between smoking and cancer. Between 1935 and 1964 scientists amassed a huge amount of evidence on the health risks of smoking. The tobacco industry loudly denied all the reports, countering with its own scientists, who routinely described all tobacco warnings as "not proven."

Physicians and antismoking lobbyists continued to argue that the tobacco companies were hiding the truth about the dangers of smoking; they also accused the companies of adding extra nicotine and other substances to make cigarettes even more addictive. In 1964 the surgeon general issued a report on the dangers of smoking; in 1966 the Federal Cigarette Labeling Act required cigarette companies to include a warning label on all cigarette packages. Lawsuits from cancer sufferers increased, but they continued to fail to convince juries that tobacco companies should be held liable.

In 1988 a lengthy court case brought to light a long-hidden document, *Motives and Incentives of Cigarette Smoking*. The confidential 1972 report, prepared by the Philip Morris Research Center, indicated that Philip Morris had been aware of the addictive nature of smoking for some time. At one point the report states, "Think of the cigarette as a dispenser for a dose of nicotine." The judge in this case found evidence of a conspiracy to conceal important consumer information by three tobacco companies, including Philip Morris, that was "vast in its scope, devious in its purpose, and devastating in its results."

Antismoking Gains Steam

Although the tobacco industry had much money at its disposal, antismoking forces were backed with reams of evidence on the dangers of smoking. Some states, California among them, began to limit smoking in public places; the federal government banned all smoking in federal buildings in 1997.

In 1997 a lawsuit was brought by the attorneys general of all 50 states, demanding compensation for the health costs of caring for millions of people suffering from tobacco-related illnesses. During the trial, another series of confidential reports was brought to light, proving that Philip Morris and other tobacco companies had knowingly conspired for decades not only to hide the dangers of smoking from the public but also to add substances to their cigarettes that made them more addictive.

In 1998 the U.S. tobacco industry agreed to a Master Settlement Agreement with 46 states (four states settled individually) to pay out $206 billion over 25 years to cover costs of Medicaid and other tobacco-related

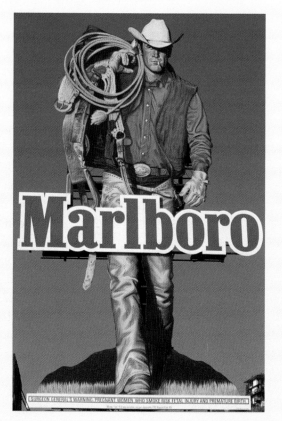

Selling Cigarettes: The Marlboro Man

Marlboro, the world's most valuable brand and the best-selling cigarette in the United States, first came to market in the 1920s. Marketers originally targeted a female audience through a series of ads in 1926 that showed a woman's hand reaching for a cigarette and used the slogan, "Mild as May." During World War II, however, Marlboro's popularity faltered and the brand was taken off the market.

Philip Morris saw its chance to reintroduce Marlboro in the early 1950s when the first studies linking cigarette smoking to lung cancer were released. Disillusioned, some consumers turned to filtered Marlboros, believing the filters made them safer. Others considered the filters to be effeminate. An advertising campaign created by the Leo Burnett Company of Chicago reintroduced Marlboro to the nation in 1955. The new campaign featured a tattooed working man. Marlboro soon became the top-selling filtered cigarette.

The "Tattooed Man" campaign used many different working men as models. The cowboy gradually emerged as the most popular character and was chosen in 1957 for a new series of ads—the Marlboro Man. In the ad, the Marlboro Man introduces himself, "I'm a rancher. Grew up in this part of the country. Own my own ranch . . . ride from one end of it to the other every day . . . I like the life a man leads out here . . . the good feeling of being your own boss. Like to smoke, too. My brand's Marlboro." By 1972 Marlboro was the top-selling cigarette in the world.

The first Marlboro Man, David McLean, and his replacement, Wayne McLaren, were both lifelong smokers. McLean died of lung cancer in 1995. His family filed a wrongful death suit against Philip Morris in 1996. In 1990 McLaren was also diagnosed with lung cancer and shortly thereafter he embarked on an antismoking campaign until his death in 1992.

Attorney Michael Piuze addresses the media in Los Angeles after a jury awarded his cancer-stricken client, Richard Boeken, more than $3 billion from Philip Morris. Behind Piuze is a diagram he used as evidence during the trial.

claims and lawsuits. Nevertheless, almost as soon as the agreement was made, the tobacco industry began to contest the amounts.

A New Challenge

In 2000 a U.S. court ordered Philip Morris and RJ Reynolds to pay a total of $20 million to a California smoker dying of lung cancer. That ruling was the first to hold cigarette makers responsible for the health of people who took up smoking after 1965, when warning labels were made compulsory on packets of cigarettes. It also opened the gates to yet more litigation. In 2001 a U.S. jury ordered Philip Morris to pay a staggering $3 billion in punitive damages to a smoker suffering terminal cancer. The jurors said they were initially partial to the tobacco giant but had been swayed by the vast amount of evidence of tobacco company conspiracy and fraud. In a separate suit in 2003, an Illinois judge fined Philip Morris $10 billion for deceptive business practices; this judgment and others were under appeal in 2003.

Public reaction to the enormous damages was varied. Many people sided with the tobacco companies, believing smoking is a personal choice, albeit an unhealthy one, made by adults. Many also felt that the settlement amounts were simply too large to be taken seriously.

Others argued that punitive damages must reflect the amount of money needed to make the company take its punishment seriously. Public opinion continues to be divided.

The legal battles over smoking are sure to continue, as Philip Morris grows larger and more diversified. In 2002 the parent company changed its name from Philip Morris to Altria Group; the operating companies, including Philip Morris USA, Philip Morris International, Miller Brewing, and Kraft Foods, will keep their names. The company claimed the name change was intended to "clarify the company identity." Others suggested it was a move to gain distance from the bad name it has earned through tobacco.

Further Reading

Glantz, Stanton A., and Edith D. Balbach. *The Tobacco War: Inside the California Battles.* Berkeley: University of California Press, 2000.

Kessler, David A. *A Question of Intent: A Great American Battle with a Deadly Industry.* New York: Public Affairs, 2001.

Kluger, Richard. *Ashes to Ashes: America's Hundred-Year Cigarette War, the Public Health, and the Unabashed Triumph of Philip Morris.* New York: Vintage Books, 1997.

Pertschuk, Michael. *Smoke in Their Eyes: Lessons in Movement Leadership.* Nashville, Tenn.: Vanderbilt University Press, 2001.

—*Lisa Magloff*

Glossary

barriers to entry Factors discouraging competition in a market.

bonds Certificates stating that a firm or government will pay the holder regular interest payments and a set sum on a specific maturity date. See encyclopedia entry, Stocks and Bonds.

capital intensity Measure of the amount of assets required to finance a given level of sales. For example, a high level of capital intensity is needed to build jet airliners.

capitalism Economic and social system based on private ownership of the means of production; goods and services are allocated through the coming together of supply and demand in the competitive free market. See encyclopedia entry.

cartel Group of producers in an industry that band together to coordinate output and prices, sometimes with government support. See encyclopedia entry.

collateral Assets used to guarantee the payment of a debt.

collective bargaining Negotiations between management and a union to establish a labor contract. See encyclopedia entry.

commodity Any natural resource or good that is traded.

comparative advantage One nation's ability to produce a good at a lower opportunity cost than can another nation. See encyclopedia entry.

contract labor Employment arrangement that specifies the work to be done, the pay rate, and so on by contract; temporary workers are contract labor. See encyclopedia entries, Labor Market; Temporary Workers.

copyright The exclusive ownership rights of authors, artists, or corporations to their works. See encyclopedia entry.

corporation Company owned by stockholders. See encyclopedia entry.

discount rate Interest rate at which banks may borrow funds for the short term from the Federal Reserve. See encyclopedia entry, Federal Reserve System.

economies of scale Declining average cost of production that results from increasing output. See encyclopedia entry.

ergonomics Science that studies how to design a tool or work environment to best fit the person using it. See encyclopedia entry.

game theory Mathematical technique used to model (and predict) the behavior of individuals and firms in markets.

inflation Period of rising prices. See encyclopedia entry.

initial public offering The first time a company sells stock to the public. See encyclopedia entry.

liquidity The ease with which assets can be converted into cash without a decline in value. See encyclopedia entry, Assets and Liabilities.

mainframe Mainframe computer; large computer that can be operated by multiple users at one time.

market share Percentage of all dollars spent on a product or service that a specific company earns for that product or service; the proportion of a particular market dominated by a specific company.

microcomputer Computer designed for personal use.

monopolistic competition Market with many producers, each of which sells its own unique product. See encyclopedia entry, Monopoly.

monopoly Type of market that involves only one seller. See encyclopedia entry.

mortgage Debt in which the borrowing business retains ownership of the property and all of its inherent liabilities. See encyclopedia entry.

mutual fund Portfolio of stocks, bonds, or cash managed by an investment company on behalf of a group of investors. See encyclopedia entry.

nationalization Government takeover of private industries.

natural monopoly Situation in which competition does not result in cheaper goods or services; instead, one firm is able to provide a good or service at lowest cost to consumers. See encyclopedia entry, Monopoly.

oligopoly Market dominated by a few sellers.

open market operations Purchase or sale of government bonds by the Federal Reserve to influence the money supply.

operating system Program for managing the software in a computer.

partnership Business structure with two or more individuals as owners. See encyclopedia entry.

patent Exclusive rights to a new product or invention for a set period. See encyclopedia entry.

pension Retirement savings plan offered through an employer.

perfect competition Theoretical market with many buyers and sellers, ease of entry and exit, and where all participants have knowledge of prices.

personal computer Computer designed for use by an individual.

philanthropy Contributing money to charitable causes.

portfolio Investments owned by a person or group.

productivity Amount of work that can be completed in a given time. See encyclopedia entry.

quota A predetermined limit on the amount of foreign goods that can enter a country.

smart card Credit-card-sized plastic card containing a microchip used for data storage and transactions.

tariff Tax on imported goods. See encyclopedia entry.

Index

Page numbers in **boldface** type indicate article titles. Page numbers in *italic* type indicate illustrations or other graphics.